The

EARTH

GAME

The

EARTH

GAME

Discovering the Cycle Inside Your Life

and

The Personal Adventure of Change

MARIANNA PORTER

CLARY PRESS

Los Angeles, California

ISBN 0-9643464-2-7

For Teresa and Joe

CONTENTS

CONTENTS, continued

All mankind is born for perfection
And each person can reach it
If he will only follow his own dharma.

— The BHAGAVAD-GITA

It Begins

I don't know how I managed before I knew how to tell what time it is.

I don't mean whether it is Tuesday or Wednesday or 4:30 or 5 o'clock. I mean what time it is in my development as a Being.

Several years ago, after studying the lives of hundreds of people, I knew that just ahead for me was a period of giving back. I had been doing research for twelve years, and that confirmation that it was time to offer up the results gave me the nerve to leave my job and publish what I have found.

And the results are clear. *We have all been set up.*

I am not sure I like that, but I see it is true. We are carried through life by a process none of us knows is there. We live our entire existence inside a cycle, and like weather, a set of changing conditions is shaping what we know.

That is a slightly disturbing realization. Still there is a sense of relief in discovering that the changes tossing us around are not just randomly cast. They occur in a regular sequence, and we can know what that sequence is.

Most of what we have already learned about change has been preserved in the community of astrologers. Now computers have opened this ancient body of knowledge to a new generation of timekeepers. Some of them are applying that knowledge to personal growth, and in this arena something amazing is going on. While we have known for a long time that each of us acquired the pattern of our star system when we were born, now we find *we are processing those patterns*. They are a sequence for our development that grows our Being the way genes grow our bodies.

Though it is not necessary to believe we have imprinted the sky in order to develop personally, as it is not necessary to believe in genes to grow up, if you knew what was happening was part of a larger design, would it make a difference? If you could see the conditions above the circumstances of your life, would you feel more in control? If you knew you were unfolding in your own right time, would making your way in the world be easier — even exciting?

So let your mind turn to the trail you are leaving behind you. It is the life we have *already* lived that will confirm that these imprints from time are real.

May you discover here the synchronous relationship between you and the solar system — ever changing, natural time.

A PLACE IN TIME

A birthprint is simply a moment in time. Our star system is a huge clock, and we measure time by the motions in it. There is the year as we circle the Sun, the month as the Moon circles us, and the day as we rotate on our own axis. In combination with the other planets, these motions create such a dizzying mix that we can differentiate any instant in our history by the pattern made when all the cycles are frozen. Every moment holds a set of conditions, and somehow when we were born we incorporated them as if adapting ourselves to fit.

Consider that we might have copied space-time the way it already exists — as a cycle of change. With ourselves at the center, we might have mapped our environment as if we, too, held a global space, perhaps casting time's topography inside us by adjusting to its qualities — each of us morphing to a slightly different set of conditions. We might have registered our position in Earth's trip around the Sun and taken note of our personal spot in its spin, each of us recording every planet and internalizing the whole pattern so completely that the conditions that appear in the day and the year appear again in us. That is what we find.

It seems we experience the same qualities that nature does, but people don't make fog in the evening or dew in the morning, and we don't make snow or grow flowers. We hold a different part of nature's continuum and manifest time in human terms — as a changing set of ideas.

Our orientation to the sky is a bit difficult to visualize, but I will give you the briefest definition of a birthprint. It is the spherical space around you, expanded to include the entire solar system at the moment of your birth, as seen from where you were born.

We experience this *personal* orb as if it had twelve sections, like the year, which the ancient astrologers called *Houses*. That is what we will call them, too, but we will include in our descriptions of them what we know today of how human beings register time. Our global identity is more than a set of characteristics holographed from our star system, as we have known for centuries. Because we process it, this imprint is a sequence for our own development. Each of us has cast a moment as a personal path, and no one else walks our piece of time. We experience its twelve ideas this way:

We place the will and project an identity.

We establish trust.

We communicate with others.

We develop a sense of Self.

We experience Being.

We cultivate mastery through the use of choice.

We become aware of how other people see us.

We shed the past and encounter dependencies.

We expand into the social network.

We recognize who we are.

We experience our autonomy.

And finally, we are delivered into a period of re-evaluation.

This is how we have registered our personal, global space. Our integration of it is the context of life, which gives even hard times a place in the whole.

PROCESSING TIME

There is no way we would know what our global space is except by discovering the qualities associated with it. With computers we can calculate the pattern for any moment in time and correlate that with everything from the stock market and politics to history and personal evolution. Because we now have the means to process huge amounts of information, it is possible to search the past and gain a global understanding of almost any subject by tracing its interaction with the changing conditions of natural time.

While astrologers with varying interests are expanding our understanding of almost every discipline this way, in the past they were people who studied the night sky — people like Ptolemy, Galileo, Kepler and Newton. We even have Galileo's calculations of his birth pattern in his own handwriting.

These people were first class thinkers, and it would not be wise to dismiss astrology as coming from an ignorance which could only flourish in a more gullible period of history. I like the story that when Edmund Halley challenged Newton's defense of astrology, Newton is said to have replied, "I have studied the subject, Mr. Halley. You have not."

Yet astrology was not on the frontier of knowledge in those days. What puts it on the leading edge in our time is the accelerated pace of change, the de-stabilizing influence that has, and our ability to search time with computers. All this is simultaneous with the transformation of our planet, and ourselves, and change is making us all seekers of a new equilibrium. Balance now depends on coming to terms with time.

The fact that we do not already realize there is a deeper spectrum to change than day and night and the seasons of the year is testament to just where we are in our development as Beings. *We are at the beginning.* We hardly know that time applies its characteristics to us as well as to the Earth. It drives our entire developmental process, and we ourselves are the experiment.

Something called the Progressing Moon taught me how this works, as studying any natural cycle would. This timer shifted the day I moved into what felt like my first real home, and the change it made was one astrologers have always associated with domestic life. That coincidence got my attention, and I began watching the Progressing Moon's cycle to see if it had a process we could track. This cycle has been my vehicle for understanding the characteristics of time. Through it I find we have indeed been touched by our star system and imprinted at birth by the pattern of a specific moment. The Progressing Moon separates the conditions we ourselves have mapped. Now we can correlate our integration of them with our individual experience of life.

That alters everything. For one thing, it marries our lives with learning. We can understand our circumstances as arising from a larger context. We can see the conditioning we carry as Beings. And for astrologers, the study of time itself becomes an experiential process.

Until now, we have had to rely on other people to interpret our patterns for us. But there is nothing in a birthprint that says how conscious a person is, and it is often difficult for an astrologer to peg an interpretation to a level right for someone else. Nor can any of us make interpretations larger than we ourselves are.

While integrating our own pattern piece by piece, however, we can understand it ourselves. We can hold past events as emanating from a specific context, and current events as part of a continuing sequence that we can know.

Great spiritual leaders have taught us we are conditioned to perceive life the way we do — that we have attitudes, opinions and positions that hinder our growth. Time delivers these conditions to us in sequence. Now we can see them and begin to separate ourselves from the qualities that color our perceptions of life.

I have set down here what the Progressing Moon has taught me about the characteristics of time, and how we interpret them and grow on this planet.

Progression

We used to refer to a locale to state who we are. Leonardo da Vinci was Leonardo from Vinci. But in a mobile society, that does not give us much information any more. Every one of us is also from a time, and it would be much more accurate to say what generation, time-of-year and time-of-day we are. That states each of us precisely, and says much more about us. These parameters define how we experience life.

After one set of conditions became resident in us at birth, like a program descending into place, we began processing it through something called progressions. Handed down to us from our timekeeper elders, progressions have always been considered a model of evolution, though I wonder how much of this they really understood. The clock continues forward inside us after we map it, but at a rate that relates two cycles. As if we had started videotaping the sky at birth, we play it forward internally from then on — so slowly it takes a whole year to play the next day. Like a very slow VCR, our holograms keep running inside, launching our development.

To understand the basis for this, be where you can view the Earth and the Sun in your mind's eye. There is the Earth rotating once around on its axis — one day — and making one trip around the Sun — one year. The motions that take place in the whole solar system during one spin of the Earth are stretched out to be the conditions we integrate during our next trip around the Sun. By the time we are ninety days old, we have ninety years of change waiting inside, wound up like a spring.

It seems to me a bit like jet lag. It takes us a while to process the changes the sky generates. In the meantime, because everything keeps on moving, we fall further and further behind. Maybe that is what aging is about. In any case, we process time much more slowly than it happens.

Though we use math to pinpoint the conditions present in any particular moment of this cycle, one-rotation-equals-one-revolution is its elegant, numberless rate. This equation changes our center of reference from the Earth to the Sun. There our lives slip into cadence with the whole planetary family. In this process we in fact mimic the Sun, first by experiencing our personal vantage point as the center of a space-time, and then by processing that space at a rate that translates a day to a year.

Perhaps our elders did not realize that because progression refers us to the centerpoint of our star system, it activates the centerpoint awareness in us. Which makes me wonder. If the Moon lets us know who *we* are through a process that refers us to the greater centerpoint of *our* system, maybe the planets let the Sun know who *it* is as it circles *its* greater centerpoint in the galaxy.

Though we calculate progressed positions for all the planets, the Moon travels the fastest and is the only body that will progress through the whole birthprint while we are still alive. It is also the only body that forms an exclusive relationship with Earth. The Moon's space contains ours, and astrologers have always associated it with containers. Even graphically it plays this role.

But the Moon does this, too, as a process. It knits our hologram together as if its name were *inclusion*, and there is an echo of elegance in that, as well. Through the Progressing Moon's cycle, we integrate the conditions in our birthprint into our memory of life so far, making a new whole of it all as we go.

In one day, the Moon in the sky moves between twelve and fifteen degrees. So starting with the Moon's position imprinted at birth, we integrate that much of our pattern over the next year. That comes down to about one degree per month. At that rate, it takes close to twenty-seven and a half years to process all 360 degrees — all twelve House partitions and every planetary placement. In a lifetime, we do that two or three times. We will be looking at personal experiences of this process.

Progressions take a lot of calculation, and we were not able to make a process of the Progressing Moon until we had computers. In the past, the calculations necessary to relate days with years were done with just pencil and paper. Though the progressed cycle was known, doing the math for more than one or two points in it took a long time. Now we are the first generation to connect the entire cycle with a life. And what a connection it makes. This cycle describes our evolution as Beings, which at the moment is going on without our conscious participation.

So both numerically and developmentally, this level of time has been waiting for our capacity to process it. We have that now. We have not only computers, but the self awareness to integrate a larger set of ideas. The Progressing Moon separates our pattern so we can see its conditions — which it delivers as qualities of consciousness.

Somehow we live in progressed time as well as in the soap opera of daily life, and a whole new portion of the spectrum is available here. We can know what kind of awareness we are integrating, and when. By tracking our inclusion of the whole sequence, we come to know who we are and develop a sense of Self. Shepherding our lives into a shape, the Progressing Moon traces our *evolving perception.*

A Personal Global Space

What I like most about doing this research is seeing how a life plays its piece of music. When we integrate a pattern, we process twelve ideas in a row, and I like to watch the lights go on in someone's mind when a memory is lit up by its place in the sequence of time. Events acquire a context.

To understand the physical foundation for a birthprint, however, look down on the Earth from high overhead. Then go to the place you were born, probably a town somewhere in the United States, and maybe not where you are now. As you approach, arrive outside so you can see the sky, and set yourself down on your back with your feet to the south as you lie down on the ground. Spread your arms out and place your palms down so you can feel the curvature of the Earth underneath.

As you rest there, divide the half sphere below you into six sections like giant slices of pie — three curving down around the Earth from your left palm, and three rising up to the right one. Now divide the sky overhead into six more — three rising up from the right palm, and three more descending down to the left.

Those are the twelve Houses. They each have a distinct and different quality, and they are always located this way — laid out from where *you* were at birth.

You are now at the center of a pattern. That is significant. In this level of time, *you* are the fixed position in the solar system, and even the Earth's roll through day and night is referenced by where you are in it.

The planetary family are somewhere in this space, too — all of them in a hoolahoop around you, sort of halfway between your feet and straight above. If you were born at night, it is dark of course, and perhaps the Moon is overhead as it was for me. This space is yours for life. It determines the context that will filter your experience. And starting with the Moon's position, it is a sequence for your development as a Being.

What time you were born makes a difference. The Earth rotates one degree every four minutes, so we change our orientation to space-time pretty fast. Two people born on the same day, in the same town, but six hours apart, have internalized very different skies.

When we release the pause button on this pattern, the Moon moves to the left through the birthprint we have now acquired, beginning our integration.

Astrologers are sometimes accused of confusing the terms that astronomers use. We tend to call everything a planet, but we do know the difference between a planet, a moon, and a star. We are concerned with the *processes* they generate, not their astronomical classifications, and in that regard they are *all* different. Because the Moon's process is *inclusion*, we know ourselves by our response to the conditions it embraces. Over a lifetime that helps us develop a sense of who we are.

I am about to give you descriptions of the Houses, but there is nothing sacred about them. These qualities have been refined by watching the experiences of hundreds of people, and I expect we will continue honing our understanding of the way each of them works.

We will look first at the concept each House carries, and then at personal experiences of how real people have integrated these ideas into their lives.

THE FIRST HOUSE

No matter where you were born, we all experience just-below-the-horizon-to-the-left in the same way. We are talking about an orientation here, and we can isolate this area now as a fixed place because it has been frozen in each of us.

From reports of processing our personal global space, we find this part of the pattern is imbued with the idea of *will*: *the ability to put your attention on something.*

Will has a point, like an arrow, and we extend it through the eyes as our point of attention. From communal space, we use this quality to focus into a body and personality.

Will is assertive. It moves outward and serves doing things: we go where our attention is.

In this condition, we express a point of view and project the external mask we display to the world. So this part of the hologram is also associated with actors.

Will is archetypally male. Though we all carry it, men emphasize projecting, doing, and steering a vehicle, which is our personal presentation in the world. Why do men like sports? Why do they compete? Why do they race cars? Why do boys like guns?

These are all examples of projecting the *will*. Even sperm are little projectiles, and this quality resonates more strongly with men.

It takes the Progressing Moon about two and a half years to integrate a House. During its passage through the First House, *will* becomes the context for pretty much everything, though we may be unaware of it. And, of course, we each express it in our own way.

When Irene began processing her First House, she was working at an advertising agency. She had been there almost ten years and liked the fast-track pace of her job. She had no trouble keeping up, until she began integrating this concept. Then episodes of exhaustion set in.

Every few weeks, for a couple of days she found she could not walk very fast. At the end of the day she would go right home to bed to recuperate, completely drained. Sometimes she missed work altogether. These periods of exhaustion became more frequent and lasted longer, until eventually she could not work at all and spent the entire next year in bed.

At that time no one even had a name for chronic fatigue, and after eight months of lying down Irene began to wonder if she would ever get well. She couldn't read and even had trouble talking because, she said, she could not focus her thoughts. Most of the time her mind just drifted.

Irene recounts that one afternoon she noticed a phrase passing through her head. "I think I have lost the will to live," she thought, and that scared her. But she says in that instant a tiny focal point appeared in her mind, and she seized it. "I made myself an imaginary cheerleader to chant Go! Go! Go! That was as much as I could put together," she said, "but that was the turning point, and I started to get better."

Feeling she had been floating for months in a half-sleep, from then on Irene made deliberate efforts to focus her attention and get back into her body. "It was like squeezing my peripheral vision into the center of my eyes."

That task is the essence of *will*. Focusing the attention through the body and out through the eyes, carrying our personal expression and laying a track for thoughts to follow behind is the pathway *will* takes through consciousness.

Eventually Irene was able to get out of bed long enough to do the humblest of chores. Slowly she steered a litany of small tasks toward getting herself up and around. "I would make up something beforehand, like moving a book from one shelf to another," she said. "I'd get a pad of paper, then go back to bed, or put out a special pen, and go back to bed again. Once in a while I could read, and sometimes I could write something down." After six months she was feeling much better.

The First House develops an awareness of the attention and its capacity to steer a life. Though she did not realize it, this is what Irene was dealing with the whole time she was in bed. The attention is the vehicle for *will* — its carrier — the same way the body is the vehicle for our Being. It is a pointer, a prow, our projective ability, and we follow where it goes first. Through her First House integration, Irene became conscious of *will* by losing and re-focusing it.

Becoming aware of your attention does not need to be such a drastic experience, of course. That was part of the special set-up in Irene's birthprint. She reports that, looking back, she had exhausted the possibilities in her job and had come to a dead end in her life. There was nothing ahead in the direction she was going. During this period she left the corporate world and turned to developing herself as an artist.

Whatever life is about, when we move into the First House we take on the added dimension of *will*. Not only did Irene become aware of having this capacity, the placement of it — where she was headed in life — became an issue.

Margot described an entirely different variation of the First House. She had spent most of her life on a spiritual quest, living for eleven years in a community that supports itself by running a spa in the California desert. But as she began integrating *will*, she also began to re-evaluate the communal lifestyle and think more about her individual potential. After years of living with others of like mind in order to practice a set of spiritual principles, she and her husband moved out to start a new life, separating from the group when she entered her First House.

Will is the capacity to separate. Though we cannot *be* separate, we can project separation, and this quality is one of our natural abilities. We would call it 'free will.'

The First House is also the most personal period of life. In it we usually experience ourselves as separate from others, and we often express that by moving. *Will* directs us to 'go out from here,' and many people choose to sever from their current situation when they process this idea. Joe moved from California back East during this time. Rose moved to Oregon. Betsy moved to Boston, and I moved to California. For all of us, this was part of wielding the quality of projection.

With the intention of reversing a deep depression, Rhonda moved while in her First House, too, but in her case in order to begin therapy. As the quality we use to present ourselves, *will* also informs the personality. If there are major blocks in the expression of who we are, this is one time they would come up. Donna also began therapy at this time, as did Diane, both of them to discover why they could not express themselves.

Paula chose this time to move to New York to study acting. So did Colleen, and this is another First House expression. Because *will* is the vehicle for consciousness, it makes us aware of having a vehicle ourselves, which is why actors resonate with this part of the birthprint. People born when planets were in this orientation — just below the left horizon — might develop acting as a profession. That was Grace Kelly's intention when she, too, moved to New York City — while in her First House.

The rest of us might temporarily try acting at this time, or simply become more conscious of our bodies. Claire had plastic surgery. "I needed a new look." Connie bought an entirely new wardrobe. "I wanted to look more like me." And for the first time in her life, Sharon decided to dye her hair blonde. Identity is the focal point other people see — the external form we project through both a body and personality.

When Valerie entered the First House, her personal appearance became a big issue. Her husband is a politician, and when he was defeated in his bid for a second term of office, it was she who was especially criticized. The voters found fault with her sense of style. By the time he ran for office again, however, she had traded her glasses for contacts, gotten a new hairdo, bought new clothes, and after seven years of marriage she had even given up using her maiden name. Opponents this time quickly accused her of changing her identity for political reasons. Yet just before that election, Valerie had entered her First House. Though she herself might have given politics as a reason, she changed her image because it was time. Even if she had been tending flowers at a cabin in the woods, she would have looked in the mirror and wanted to do something different. The First House makes all of us aware of how we present ourselves.

Margaret has been a spiritual teacher for most of her seventy-five years, and she speaks publicly about aligning the personality with Soul. But while integrating her First House, she began to put more emphasis on her personal expression. Within two months of entering this part of her birthprint, and to the surprise of many who knew her, she gave an elegant luncheon for close to a hundred people as "a celebration of the personality." After years of teaching the value of identifying with spirit, this seemed to be a change in direction. Yet even within a life devoted to soul awareness, there is a time to emphasize your own personality, and the First House is it. In fact, shortly after that, she moved, too.

Sometimes we translate these qualities so directly that the very word for a concept shows up one's life. My mother made a translation like that. After her husband died she became matriarch to the two families of children woven together when she and her husband married in their retirement. So as not to offend anyone while allocating the family property, she wrote to her husband's children and asked each of them what they would like to inherit when she died. Sorting and tagging the furniture, she spent her First House *writing her will*.

These examples are typical of how the characteristics of time appear in a life. But they are rationalizations, really, of our larger education. The changing context that results from processing our own birthprint eventually induces a greater understanding of who we are — and often of who we are not.

Ultimately, aligning the *will* with our Being is its most harmonious placement. Though it may seem productive at first and perhaps serve discovering what does *not* work, all other projections eventually meet only resistance.

That human beings walk blithely around inside a set of ideas that seem to be part of our orientation to the star system is just astonishing. How did anyone ever discover that? Maybe mothers noticed children born at the same time of day had similar ways. Maybe shepherds thought a lot about the sky and the planets. Maybe alien beings came down in spaceships and taught us the whole thing and then left. No one recorded who originally thought of correlating traits with the sky. But we can *know* that conditions associate with birthprints by personally experiencing our own.

THE SECOND HOUSE

I didn't realize until years after I began tracking the Progressing Moon that it would make a bigger picture, so I did not record the early examples of this cycle, and not every aspect of an energy will be illustrated. Nor could they be, since we each express the same idea in a different way. But there are enough illustrations here to confirm that something fascinating is going on.

Real experiences are the best way to understand the qualities of time. Its characteristics show up in all kinds of ways, but if you know what you are looking at, you will be able to recognize a concept while you are dealing with it as it passes through your life.

Whereas the First House spotlights some aspect of the attention and usually involves a re-focusing, the Second House is about stabilizing that new beginning. Circling left below the horizon, the second partition down has imprinted the quality of *trust: stability, confidence, commitment and havingness.*

This is our basic experience of sufficiency. Do I *have* enough, and am I *myself* enough. Here we experience worth and self confidence. From this part of the pattern we derive value and self esteem. All of these are forms of havingness, and in various ways we establish a sense of ownership here. In physical reality we translate this to food, money and possessions.

Some people process the Second House around having the material things necessary for a stable life. As the means for acquiring them, of course money is part of that equation, which was the situation for Janice.

Janice began dating someone seventeen years younger than she when she entered her Second House, and the two of them formed a partnership to write music together. She saw him as a catalyst for getting her career going in the entertainment business. But he did not contribute financially, so to support themselves they spent her savings and put their expenses on her credit cards.

Eventually their business dried up, and she took a minimum wage job at a convalescent home to pay the rent. When the two of them split up a year later, he left her with their debts, and she had to declare bankruptcy. "I felt like a fool for trusting him," she said. "Creditors were calling me at work. Sometimes I even borrowed money from petty cash to buy gas for the car so I could get home." Her self esteem plunged.

The internal experience of *trust* is self esteem — how much we trust that we ourselves are enough. Janice spent more money than she had to maintain this relationship. Though it was initially about money, integrating the Second House eventually exposed her level of self worth. She herself says that that was the lesson.

Money offers the same kind of stability in the physical world that we experience in ourselves as confidence. That both show up while integrating the Second House is confirmation that these two really are intertwined. They are both rooted in the sense of *trust*.

Nancy, too, found the bottom-line on her self esteem while in the Second House. "Oh, that was a major relationship, and it was bad," she said. When I asked her to elaborate, she described this time for its effect on her confidence. "I was going out with someone who couldn't decide between me and his old girlfriend. He even slept with her while we were having a party at the house, and everyone knew what they were doing. It was horrible, but still I couldn't break up with him."

Nancy's pattern puts a heavy emphasis on this House. She was born when planets were in this part of her sky, and as she integrated it, a lifelong issue of confidence came to the surface in full force. She went on to relate that at one point the old girlfriend kicked down her front door and attacked her in front of this man while he did nothing to stop her. "I even got VD from him. We argued, and when he hit me I tried to make my black eye worse so I could dislike him enough to leave," she said.

With the deepest planetary processes affecting her ability to trust herself, we could anticipate that Nancy would also plumb the depths of self esteem in this part of her life. She was already set up to take a sounding on it, and it would have come up somehow, no matter what she was doing. As she progressed to the end of this part of her birthprint, she was able to break off that relationship.

Lydia processed her Second House around the idea of money, too. She had married a very wealthy older man, but they were not compatible and they drifted apart before he died. Though he had left her a large sum, she was experiencing her own self worth at the time of his death and began battling her dead husband's family for a greater share of his money. Pressing this issue was her way of integrating the idea of *trust*.

We place a value on whatever gives us stability, whether that is currency, possessions, or ideas, and the Second House brings up the whole issue of values. Michael entered his Second House while he was running for political office, and his message immediately changed. "New value systems are needed more than ever before," he began repeating. But of course, now he would think so.

It is *trust* that provides our capacity for commitment, and these two have a direct relationship. The more trust we have, the more we can commit. I know commitment was a factor in the life of a dear friend of mine. She talked often about not wanting to be here, and some time ago she committed suicide. Years later I went back to calculate her birthprint. She had major energy in her Second House and was integrating it when she died. Born premature, she probably fought hard to stay alive, and I wonder if she was replaying those first feelings of instability while integrating this part of her pattern. Maybe as a preemie she found living too difficult and could not quite commit to being here. While I knew her she frequently mentioned killing herself, but it came up more often as *trust* became the context for everything.

Julia also has major energy in her Second House, and this is her second time through it. I asked her about the first one. "I was married then. It was really hard, and I feel the same way now. I don't feel good about myself again." As she talked and linked both those periods to her level of confidence, her voice changed and I could tell she had gotten a handle on it.

If you can hold a difficult time as part of the larger cycle, it can lighten up. Knowing the quality you are dealing with offers a way to hold your experience of it, even if it's bad.

Personal Holidays

If the birth time on your birth certificate is accurate, we can pinpoint the days you move from House to House throughout a lifetime. These are your personal holidays. Only you have them. These events in time occur only every couple of years, so they are less frequent than birthdays.

These special days are exciting to celebrate because they mark real changes. Moving from one idea into another is like tuning to a different kind of space, and taking time out to make the switch more conscious is fun.

Or don't celebrate them. But do watch these passages. Over the years you will be able to see them for the changes in context they are.

THE THIRD HOUSE

When asked to recall a particular year or month, people tend to pick out incidents that illustrate the condition they were moving through at the time. As we process a concept, events that demonstrate that quality are the ones we seem to remember as significant.

That makes me wonder what 'significance' is. Maybe it is our resonance with time. We find that experiences that exhibit its changing conditions register more deeply. It may be that meaning itself is a function of experiencing our own path.

One friend of mine vividly recalls a specific scene from her childhood. She remembers saying to her parents when she was nine years old, "Words are a barrier." Wondering why she would remember that one phrase so clearly, we quickly referred to her timeline. She was processing *communication* that entire year. Forty years later, she still remembers this one comment.

Communication is processed in the third partition in the lower hemisphere, almost directly in back of us as we imprinted the space around us.

We associate this area with reading, writing and discussion, students, schools and libraries. We manifest it in newspapers, correspondence, neighborhoods, associations, commerce, communi-

ty, diversity and cities, and in our connection to the local environment. Children associate it with siblings. And it is the nervous
system that performs the function of *communication* in the body.

This is the quality we use to assimilate the ways of our
culture when we go to school. We experience it internally when we
make the mental connections necessary to learn. It makes for being
a student.

Isabel became a student again at the age of thirty-seven while
integrating her Third House. She began meeting privately with a
spiritual teacher twice every week. She also read widely during that
part of her life to find what she described as 'her place in the
world.' That is an adult version of connecting with the cultural
environment delivered to us as children in school.

Children also use this condition to assimilate into their local
environment — the family — and it is fascinating to see how
siblings experience this idea as adults. Though she was fifty-four
years old, Kim felt the need to re-connect with her sister when she
entered this House. The two of them spent their first time alone
together since childhood taking a trip to Disneyland.

Passing through this concept sets us up to re-establish
communication in whatever form is suitable. Often a sense of
community becomes important. To keep her relatives in touch
with each other, Brenda began writing a family newsletter in her
Third House. Ethel launched a monthly publication to comment
on current events. Mike revived a lifelong interest in ham radio,
and Antoinette took a job as an editor at a publishing house. All
these are experiences of communication and its function in creating
community.

Travelling locally is an external form of *communication*, and
the Indian sage Ramakrishna spent this time on a pilgrimage to the
major holy places in northwest India.

This quality also disposes us to create communities ourselves
and form associations with others. It brings information from the
local environment, and we use it to contribute our own thoughts.

Libraries are probably full of Third House types of people, as well as the phone company, newspapers and the post office. By that I mean people who had planets in a Third House orientation when they were born. When we imprint planets in a particular House, they add an emphasis of that idea because we process them, too, and in terms of that House's concept.

As the basis for the way we experience the world, birth patterns can help us sort out why we feel the way we do and how long a particular interest is likely to last. Astrologers do this kind of research for fun. Most of my research has been to discover the expression of this cycle in one life, but any teacher could study its effects across a classroom of students. Spending two and a half years in one quality is a long time when you are a child, but a child's perception of the world occasionally changes, too. It is important for teachers to realize that. A lot depends on the part of the birthprint a child is integrating, and children having problems may be processing a condition that is difficult for them.

Studying children in the classroom is just brimming with potential. For example, what correlation does learning to read have with the House a child is processing? What's happening with children who have attention deficit syndrome or dyslexia? What about aggressive children? What about children who suddenly withdraw? Over the twelve years we are in school, we all do better or worse in different grades, and sometimes we remember one period when everything seemed to go right. Why is that? I distinctly remember liking the summer after my Seventh Grade when a few friends and I explored our small town on our bikes. I guess that was my half-adult version of travelling. I was in my Third House that year.

In the stretch of a whole life, the local events that resonate with the birthprint become part of our memory. They take their place in the landscape of our dynamic marathon through time, all of it run in slow motion.

THE FOURTH HOUSE

The Fourth House marks a way station on the path. In a private way, something gels here. This quality confers a shape on the experience of who we are.

While we absorb life's changing conditions, we develop an interior reservoir of experience. The Fourth House condition receives new events, integrates them into our past, and forms a sense of Self. From directly in back, in the area rising up toward the right, we experience *Self perception: a single, unified awareness.* Even this reference for who we are to ourselves alone speaks when it is ready, and not before.

The Fourth House registers in the form of feelings: this feels good, that doesn't, this is me, that is not. Yet this condition holds much more than feelings. It shapes our integrity and determines our perception.

House by House, planet by planet, and frequency by frequency, it is precisely this interior reservoir that stores our integration of time. This House is our personal memory bank of how life has been so far. Holding our memories and habits, it forms an internal sense of home and is our reference for what a home is. In total, the Fourth House is our capacity to hold a space, and eventually to know who we are. Mothers occupy this space until we separate from them. They hold who we are first, and they are the Fourth House archetype.

The internal sense of Self is reflected in how we perceive the external world as well. We project who we feel we are onto family and ancestors, and onto where we live. The energy in this part of the pattern even colors our taste in home decor.

Because I knew Deanna had recently entered her Fourth House, I asked her what she was doing. She had just returned from a forty-day retreat in the desert with a master teacher, and when I inquired about the specifics, she replied, "It was about the experience of Self." In the fifteen years I have known her, I never heard her refer to the Self until she processed this part of her pattern and became interested in who she is inside.

In her Fourth House, Veronica, too, had experiences relating to her sense of Self. Unlike most people, she found a career early in life and seemed to have no trouble establishing a reputation as a designer. Her life was running smoothly on the outside, but when I talked to her, she said *she doesn't know who she is.* Her pattern puts an emphasis on increasing Fourth House consciousness, so to understand how that is happening I asked her to talk about what I knew was her first Fourth House experience.

For some people this happens early in life, and Veronica was just seventeen years old the first time she processed this part of her birthprint. "I was doing huge stage sets for a play in high school, and that's when I felt the first connection with myself as an artist. I remember a real feeling of self satisfaction," she said.

I hadn't told her she was developing self awareness during those years, yet in remembering them she referred directly to that kind of experience.

Though lots of things happen in the span of a House, when we look back, those experiences that resonate with this cycle accumulate a special kind of knowledge. We could call it *wisdom.* And as the result of integrating changing conditions, physicists might recognize this process for its similarity to the theory of chaos. In consciousness, as well, we are always forming a new whole inside.

Since her high school days, Veronica has had a career as an animation artist, but her sense of Self took center stage again when she integrated the Fourth House a second time twenty-seven years later. "I had a love affair with a pen pal that year. It was wonderful, he made me feel good about myself."

Though a pen pal may seem to be a remote way of increasing self awareness, this is a subtle, yet firm, process. There were very few times when Veronica indeed *did* feel good about herself, but this was one of them. When I asked her to recall the Fourth House period, she went directly to the experience of Self again. Her significant memories rang true to the idea she was processing at the time.

Since we refer to this quality for our idea of 'home,' it brings up the whole idea of having one. For some people, that is a reason to get married. After a successful career, Rita got married when she entered her Fourth House. "I needed to be home more," she said. I know of four other people who have married here for that reason.

As a teacher who gives seminars in cities around the country, in his Fourth House it became important to James to have an anchor in life. He found this the appropriate time to move in with his girlfriend in order to have a home base for his travels.

After more than ten years of royal duties, upon entering her Fourth House Princess Diana announced she was stepping out of the public eye in order to spend more time at home with her sons. Even people who live very public lives feel the need for this private space in time. It is a period of internal awareness that promotes an experience of who we are.

Of course I know my own life best, so I will tell you my Fourth House stories. I was just eleven years old the first time through this part of my birthprint, and I was at summer camp in the Wisconsin north woods. My mother was a teacher and was not paid over the summer, so she took a job as a camp counselor and her compensation was that my sister and I could attend as campers for free. I was acutely aware at that age of being an outsider amongst the daughters of wealthy Chicago families who regularly spent summers there, and I did not like camp at all. But during those eight weeks I moved into my Fourth House. I remember one specific evening at the main lodge at the end of the summer. I was sitting at the dinner table dreaming of going home when I heard the camp director call my name from the stage. I was being summoned to the front to receive an award as best camper of the year. I didn't think anyone had even noticed me. As I look back, that night marks the first time I noticed myself. It was like a ripple arriving at my shore.

During the second time through my Fourth House I moved into the apartment I live in now. That was before I started studying this cycle, and I experienced it this time as a new home. But it was also something else. As I was unpacking my things, I put a stack of papers on my desk to sort out and put away later, and I noticed on top was a printout I had ordered from a computer service listing the calculations called progressions. That day was listed there, and I leaned over to see why. The Moon in my pattern had just progressed into my Fourth House. It was during that passage that I slowly began to realize the Moon integrates, that perception is its process, and that over a lifetime we experience this process as an evolving *Self perception*.

So I understood the Fourth House process while in the Fourth House myself. How does that happen? From that time on I wanted to know the rest of this cycle. I listened to people tell their stories, and the Progressing Moon began teaching me what time is about.

The Biography of the Future

Last night I saw a panel of biographers discussing their craft around a table on late-night television.

"We all have a hunger to see our lives in a longer view," one of them remarked when asked why he wrote biographies. He has no idea what is in store for that profession.

Since I first realized what is going on with the Progressing Moon, I have been keeping notes of my experiences so that in my old age I can write my story in terms of time. The education of the spirit *is* the longer view, and the sky dictates the order in which that education takes place. We do not have the slightest inkling of how clearly the cosmic path guides our growth and ensures that we study all the subjects.

I look forward to reading the autobiographies of people who can see their own process. And for historical figures, time is going to be a fascinating addition to the tools biographers use to understand people long dead. The way in which we process our birth-print is everybody's story.

THE FIFTH HOUSE

We are more available to the evolution carried in the Moon's cycle than ever before. Amongst other things, the Moon's process is the repository for feelings, and over the last hundred years, with the development of psychology, we have begun to tone down the clamor from the emotional system. Psychological counseling is pretty widely available for anyone who finds the past too heavy to carry, and by that advancement alone we have more sensitivity available for the Moon's larger capacity for Self.

Coupled with other forms of self awareness, understanding the basic dynamic of withholding and expressing emotions has liberated an observer in us that is not totally consumed by feelings. Now we can have our feelings without being overwhelmed by them, and this slightly increased capacity is student to a larger education. The here-and-now is necessary for this part of our development. To the degree that we are not attached to the past, we can be at home in the present, and the Fifth House develops expressing who we are. From the second of three sections moving up toward the right we experience self expression, or *creativity*. In full flower, this part of the birthprint is *self actualization*.

This quality comes from the centerpoint awareness that mimics the Sun. It is sovereign and self-governing. In this condition we play, perform, have courage and simple strength of Being. The Fifth House is our reference for valor and nobility. It activates heartspace, and children live here.

But the primary creation emanating from the ability to express ourselves is behavior — we all create that. With the inclusion of all our traits, behavior is our first experience of self actualization.

Royalty hold the Fifth House archetype. As the figures at the center around which court life revolves, they demonstrate the centerpoint as a cultural phenomenon. In a kingdom, life revolves around the King. Yet in time, in the solar system, each of us holds a global reality, and that makes centerpoints of us all. We are all royal in the theater of time. At the center of a holographed sky, we are at the heart of a process, which is royalty's modus operandi.

Though in the end we are cultivating creativity, because the centerpoint lights up our heartspace, sometimes a lover appears at this time. Esther fell in love with a man carrying a lot of Fifth House energy himself when she processed this part of her field. When he invited her to attend a class studying the creative process, she joined him at a weekly gathering assembled to discuss the metaphysics of creating a life. "That's when my heart opened up," she said. "I felt it in my chest. And he was the reason I went to those classes." Esther described this time as an explosion that released a terrific need to express herself. Her heartspace was called open by this relationship, but it was occupied by the creative process. After that she began a career as a writer.

During her Fifth House, Carol enrolled in a ceramics class. She bought a potter's wheel, found a place to store it, and for the remainder of this phase, she wrapped her life around making pots.

Corrinne began writing poetry. Though she had thought about language for most of her life, it was not until she reached her Fifth House that she began putting her ideas into poems. Here she developed a piece that she says "expresses who I really am." That's a Fifth House experience of self actualization.

Franklin D. Roosevelt created a center for polio patients while in his Fifth House. He came down with polio in 1921, before he was President, and because he needed physical therapy, he developed a spa in Warm Springs, Georgia where he and other people with polio-weakened muscles could exercise and encourage each other. Biographers describe this period as "a remarkably inventive time." Warm Springs was itself his creation, but there he also designed braces, crutches, and a muscle testing technique that is still in use today. He used this part of his life to express a blossoming creativity.

Michael went prospecting for gold in the California mountains when he entered this part of his pattern. Gold and royalty both associate with the centerpoint awareness, and throughout history we have correlated gold with kings. The British even called their gold coin a *sovereign*. Gold is a noble metal, it is incorruptible, and it resonates with the incorruptibility of the centerpoint in us, our Being. Michael never looked for gold before. It was a local experience of time.

For some people the creative process is an intellectual one, perhaps completely invisible to others. An internal and quiet sort of person, Albert Einstein was busy developing his theory of relativity while in his Fifth House.

But creativity is not reserved for special people. It is a time for stating all our capacities together as one expression — not doing, but being. Creativity is available to anyone who can be conscious in present time.

Your pattern is beautifully specific. No one else knows your experience, nor the nuances of it you have stored inside. No one else senses the internal reverberations set off by changing conditions, nor the new paradigms generated by them. You are the only witness to a unique set of characteristics, and in the Fifth House you *be* them.

THE SIXTH HOUSE

By the time you reach the Sixth House you have been through about twelve years of personal development. Whether you think so or not, you have been educated about *will, trust, communication, self perception* and *creativity.*

Though we do not spend all our attention on an idea as we pass through it, we absorb it somehow. When its time comes, we learn about a quality whether we accept or reject it, and in the Sixth House, choosing, itself, becomes the lesson.

By this time we have ignition in the heart, the fire has been lit, the engine turned on, and now we tend the flames. A little less fuel, a little more air, an adjustment here and there — from just below the horizon to the right, through the last partition in the lower hemisphere we exercise *choice.* Yes-no, right-left, on-off, up-down, here we apply ourselves to something as one functioning unit.

This faculty operates like a shake-down cruise. The Sixth House aims for efficiency, and this condition usually illuminates what does *not* work. Through analysis and critique, by making assessments and adjustments, this part of the birthprint develops a facility for discernment.

In the body this characteristic manifests our state of health. By selecting from the nutrients we ingest, the body chooses what it needs to maintain itself, and we have known for a long time that health relates to this part of the pattern.

We might become aware of fitness here. Having no interest in diet before, when David entered his Sixth House he started reading about how to eat right, and within weeks he took to growing sprouts in his kitchen. He and his partner Brenda are synchronized — their Moons progress from House to House at about the same time. Several months later, as she entered her Sixth, they both immersed themselves in the Indian philosophy of diet.

In the external application of this idea, however, we choose how to spend our time. In our culture we do that primarily through work. On a daily basis we process something at our jobs, whether that is information, a piece in the manufacture or distribution of a product, orders for it, or perhaps we are just processing time. Day in and day out, we sort the ongoing flow of energy through the work we do, and the work world has been the forum for cultivating *choice* for hundreds of years now.

This capacity is critical for our development. As difficult as it may be for parents, "What do you want to do when you grow up?" is a decision we instinctively leave up to the child. We all must learn to steer a course through life. The ability to project ourselves, a profound trust in life, facile communication, a defined sense of Self, and the freedom to create — all remain incomplete until we are tuned up and applied to something. We need right work, though perhaps not in the form of a job. At some point in our development, we apply choice to expressing who we are.

After spending twelve years moving through the lower hemisphere, if your current work was ever right, it is probably not right any more. In an historical period moving as fast as this one, we are likely to outgrow what we do for a living more than once, and that fact may become apparent while we are processing *choice*. People are often laid off or change jobs in the Sixth House.

Annie was let go from her job selling advertising space for a newspaper, and she went through three more sales positions while integrating this part of her pattern, quitting one of them herself.

Karen realized she could not reconcile her own values with the goals of a media monitoring group she was working for, and while sorting this out in her Sixth House, she was laid off.

After eleven years at a major corporation doing something she had lost interest in, Janet, too, was let go in this House as her company reduced its staff.

A few people, however, seem to tune right in on this condition and choose a new routine before one is chosen for them. Gordon decided he could no longer build special effects for an entertainment company while in his Sixth House and struck out on his own as an artist. It seems that how he spent his time became more important while he was integrating the ability to choose.

The Sixth House is our apprenticeship to dancing lightly from yes to no as we see fit, tuning ourselves up in a push toward mastery. As a rudder for directing the flow of energy, *choice* is the technique of living, and to be a Master is to choose so easily and so well that the flow of energy and time is continual in the body, and in life. The ability to choose our way through the day completes our personal development, and when we are humming with efficiency, health and right work, we ourselves are the masterpiece.

We might call *choice*, processing. Pat joined a group to process what was blocking her from success as an actress. While in this part of her life, she enrolled in a course set up to goose the participants into their chosen careers. Margaret underwent a complete series of Rolfing sessions to process the energy jams in her body. And Ivy began a spiritual discipline designed around processing frequencies through meditation. All these practices are about processing, which we experience as *choice*.

Judy was born with several planets in a Sixth House orientation, and she was referring to this part of her pattern when she described how she readies a piece of performance art. "My mind seems to flicker like frames of movie film passing through a camera. Honing a piece feels like tightening up the frequency of the flicker, making it sharp and precise." Whether we are built to emphasize this condition all the time, or to experience it for only the short period we integrate this House, the fine tuning we do in life is an exercise in the delicate use of *choice*.

Eric works at a radio station, and during his Sixth House he began installing new wallboard in the broadcast studio. He told me that figuring out just what was needed to improve the quality of sound required a lot of tinkering. I asked if 'tuning up the room' was an accurate description, and he thought it was. Next he figured out how to change the wiring to make the whole station operate better. Whether we apply it to our environment, our thoughts, or our body, tuning up is a Sixth House function.

People who are born with planets here are often good at fixing things. One of my brothers was born with the Moon in this part of his sky, and he built his car by taking apart two others. He likes to have some sort of project going at all times and has now built and landscaped his own home. He is a natural fixer-upper: process, process, process.

What we are built to do and how well we function are developed through the Sixth House experience. Every manifested instant is valid and necessary for Earth's full expression of time, but since we embody only our particular place and moment, we need others to play their parts, too. It turns out each person's role is felt by the rest of us as service. No one can perform another's work, so we are quite happy when someone does it well. I always thought service meant selling pencils on a street corner for Jesus, and I was not too keen on it. But since each packaged moment is unique, no one else manifests our combination of qualities, and to choose well is to contribute them in good working order. Rather than the expected drudgery, service is the natural result of mastering *choice* while contributing who we are.

Our state of health and our daily routine both emanate from this kind of consciousness. *Choice* is health incarnate and the fluid use of time, and through this condition we have the potential of achieving perfection.

The Seventh House

If we were already Masters I suppose we wouldn't be here. Earth is a perfect setup for apprentices. Its polar existence requires that we make choices — up-down, give-take, stay-go, express-withhold. Navigating our way through pairs of opposites is built into staying alive on this planet.

By the completion of our personal development in the lower hemisphere, however, whatever choices we have made, whoever we have become, it all begins to show publicly as we enter the Seventh House.

Just as night and day are, the hemispheres are different. They imprint us with two different sets of characteristics. The lower hemisphere imprints qualities of personal development, and though they may involve public experiences, *will, trust, communication, Self perception, creativity* and *choice* are developed primarily through personal, not public, life.

But spread across the sky overhead, the six Houses in the upper hemisphere carry qualities developed socially with others. The public world is an altogether different arena, and it begins in the Seventh House.

Having completed our private formation, in this House we receive feedback from the world. The Seventh bears the space of relationship, and our fourteen-year education in the public arena begins with *reflection* from someone else.

Since time colors both our external and internal experiences, in this condition we could either *do* the reflecting or *be* reflected.

To reflect is to be a sounding board, to listen actively, to receive others, and to harmonize or balance two points of view. To *be* reflected is to become an object of attention. In both cases, this House is an experience of *other*.

Sexual relationships are a common way to process this condition, and it is often a love interest who does the reflecting. Rebecca was seventeen years old the first time through this part of her pattern, and high school was about her boyfriend. "He was the first person who saw me as I am." She doesn't remember much else. Having a boyfriend may seem an obvious memory of that age, but not everyone recalls high school that way. For some people those years turn on academic success, or total invisibility, or being sick with polio. A lot depends on what part of the pattern we are in at the time. Rebecca felt seen, and she was in the Seventh House mode of receiving attention.

Astrologers refer to this part of the pattern for information about relationships. John got married in the Seventh House. So did Peter. In mid-life Desireé had her first relationship with a man, and this is a common way to experience *reflection*.

As we mature, however, public feedback often comes from a larger arena than coupledom. At the beginning of his second trip through this House, Clark had just published his first story, and very soon he began receiving comments from readers. At this stage in his life, they were his public echo. He encountered his reflection in the world, too, but in a way quite different from pairing up with another person.

After years as a corporate executive, John's Seventh House added a public dimension to his life, too. As the CEO of a large company, his philanthropy and a growing willingness to take part in civic affairs began carrying him into a more social life. The community now became his mirror. Though he had been a highly successful businessman for many years, while processing *reflection* he became a public figure.

If an emphasis on this part of your pattern makes the Seventh House an abiding condition — if you were born when there were planets in the sky just above the horizon to your right — *reflection* will bring up special issues, as it did for Clara. She describes an ever-present feeling that she is not heard by those around her. Eventually she became the mother of a profoundly deaf son. When he was born, not being heard became a fact of life. But she did not address this issue until she reached her Seventh House. Though her son was several years old by then, suddenly she was extremely uncomfortable with the attention they drew while learning to communicate in sign language. Here she learned to deal with the way other people responded to her. "I had to if we were going to communicate," she said.

Louise also carries strong Seventh House energy, and she had a similar experience. With symptoms recently diagnosed as multiple sclerosis, when she entered this House, she, too, began coping with public attention — in her case because she was in a wheelchair. "At first I was embarrassed," she said, "but that experience forced me to deal with how other people see me. I found most people were actually very helpful." Due to recent techniques for generating new neural pathways, Louise has been up and walking again for years — but not before fielding responses from the public in the Seventh House part of her life.

With strong energy in his Seventh, sound and listening were part of Alexander Graham Bell's development, too. Sound is a basic form of receiving energy, the Seventh House mode, and he also had lifelong experiences with deafness. His mother was deaf, and he became a teacher to deaf children, so he wasn't heard either. That condition became the catalyst for an historic insight. When he entered his Seventh House, he realized sound could be transmitted by wire. His experiences with hearing came to fruition, and because he was concerned with sound, we got the telephone.

By the time she arrived at her Seventh, Lorraine had spent years in an abusive relationship that she was unwilling to give up. But when the natural course of life drew her into considering just how she was being received, the quality of their relationship became important and she was able to break things off. Painful and enduring issues like this are addressed in their own right time, as part of our evolutionary process. While Lorraine was not happy with this man, she was not focused on that fact until *reflection* brought their relationship into high relief.

The Seventh House can also be quite a different kind of experience. As an expression of mirroring someone else, sometimes it just makes you want to dance. Brenda took dance lessons here for the only time in her life.

Mirroring others became important for this woman, too, in yet another fashion. Noreen lived communally in order to follow a spiritual discipline, and in her Seventh House she became a sounding board to facilitate others in her community. During that time she developed what she calls being 'an honorable adversary.' In order to clarify issues that other members of the community were dealing with, she presented the reverse point of view. In just that fashion, the Seventh House has traditionally been associated with opposition. Opponents are an experience of "other."

The Moon was setting when Lily was born, so she experiences the world in a Seventh House way all the time. She is keenly aware of sound and continually hears double meanings in words. "Some people see double," she says, "I hear double." So hers is another Seventh House experience of sound. When she hears a word, in her mind she often hears two interpretations of it at the same time. She delights in sounds that express opposite associations. "Like pray and prey," she said. "They sound the same, but they have opposite meanings. I have always been like this." That continual perception of opposites is the way of a Seventh House Moon.

Though again we all carry it, and anyone with a Seventh House emphasis will express it all the time, women hold this archetype. They are the receptive gender biologically. Generally, women are more interested in relationships than men. They are credited with being the better listeners and are sensitive to whether their partners listen to them. Emphasizing the body part that receives sound, women even decorate their ears.

Whatever your pattern is, we all become aware of *reflection* in the Seventh House part of life. Some people make or break a relationship here; some confront a fear of being looked at; some resolve issues about being heard, while others elicit a flare for balance or an ear for metaphor. The Seventh House lessons will be as unique as we are, but encountering a complement in the world is our common initiation into the upper hemisphere of the pattern, the public arena of life.

We digest each of these qualities over a period of years, and they are more important for what matures inside us through our integration of them than for the circumstances they generate. Though the resulting dramas are most entertaining, it is not the soap opera of life that we remember when we die. We depart this world with some greater knowledge of Self, garnered from our experience of time.

THE EIGHTH HOUSE

If our biology has a timetable, and our social development has a timetable, it appears the education of our Being does, too. It is visible in the events to which we give meaning, and those correlate with time.

That meaning, however, can be packed into one major event. When people recall a piece of time, that is often the case, though we spend several years taking in a concept. Maybe as we wade into a quality, our awareness suddenly snaps into synchrony with it. However this works, the conditions of time eventually show up in our lives, and the Eighth House condition can be a difficult one.

In the course of a life, this House makes a big impression. Here we cross some sort of 'event horizon' and enter into crucible conditions. This space behaves as if it is collapsing from one state into another, forsaking the past for the present. Moving upward from the right, in the Eighth House we brave the cryptic quality of *power: the ability to let go of the old.*

In real time, a new context is always arising, and *power* derives from our ability to stay current with changing conditions. It demands that we release our attention from even those things that cause us pain. The Eighth House is a mutating space, and here we must drop the embellishments that belong to the past.

Usually this means we suffer painful demonstrations of our attachments. When faced with either letting go or being ripped from the old, almost all of us are torn. Our attention is at stake here, and to some degree it is stuck to something. It normally takes a crisis to bring it back.

Inducing an implosion to some destination with which we are not familiar yet, *power* has the feeling of the inevitable taking over as it does in birth and death. Desire, jealousy, envy and obsession light up just what we are attached *to* as the moving front presses us away from the old and into the core of our Being. With no room for deadwood, what belongs in the past is surrendered now as we transmute our way through this condition. Mothers know this process when they birth babies, and all of us move through it when we die. The Eighth House generates a new space — it is evolution itself.

Since most of us are operating on learner's permits here, this quality often clarifies how much power we have given away. Through our attachments, the Eighth House reveals our dependencies, and this process pushes us to abandon them, usually unwillingly. Since no excess baggage passes through this black hole in time, we are confronted with what we must leave behind, and if we are bound to it, *it hurts*.

But it doesn't need to. We do not have to be dragged into this re-birth backwards and unconscious like a breech baby. Dealing with *power* means disengaging from the old and re-aligning with our center where a fusion is taking place. Not who we were, but who we have become is born now, on the edge of loss and in the exhilaration of being alive. Our accrued development is called home — all of it. Collected dependencies, unaddressed issues, accumulated attachments, debts, our frayed edges, and our growth — it all fuses together as the Eighth House drives everything inward toward a new synthesis. At our core, what is mature becomes strong enough to take right action without regard to consequence.

People with an emphasis on the Eighth House are the risk-takers of the world — the bungee jumpers, enthusiasts of "extreme" sports, and emergency room workers. These people experience an intensity inside which they seek to recreate through the kind of immediacy that exists at the edge between life and death.

Passage through the Eighth House can bring experiences with actual physical death as well. My mother died at the very end of my Eighth House. In its external expression, too, the past collapses inward and a life collects for passage on, including elements requiring re-dress. Accounts are brought up for closure, the space closes down, and some find a welcome release in dropping what they no longer wish to carry. Death is a condensed version of the transformation at the bottom of *power*, in which even the physical body is left behind.

Death and the force that generates life are opposite poles of the same process. From giving up the physical body altogether to spawning a new one, *power* resonates with sex as well as death. Like this. Martin had always considered himself a laggard because at twenty-two he still hadn't any sexual experience. But he entered his Eighth House that year, and within months he had his first encounter. No late-bloomer at all, he was simply responding to his own internal cycle.

Elaine became sexually involved the year she, too, entered her Eighth House, though she was only fifteen years old. So did Helen at nineteen. Whether it is wise or not, sex is a frequent experience of *power* on the first go-round. The energy at the core of Being is calling for our attention.

And it will have our attention one way or another, no matter how old we are. Mary was only two the first time she experienced this part of her pattern, and though she cannot recall any events, she has disturbing feelings associated with that age. She could be remembering the sensation of the energy itself, or by resonance, that time could have induced events involving other people as well. She fears she was molested. How would another person know what energy she was processing? I think we would call it chemistry. It is probably what the East calls karma. One energy resonates with itself-in-another, and hers could have called up issues of dominance and power in someone else if it were strong enough in them both.

At age thirty-three, Terry was making his second trip through the Eighth House when turbulent power struggles erupted between him and his wife. She threw all his things onto the lawn, and he stole her stereo system. She took some of his belongings in revenge, and he took some more of hers. During this period he lost her, his home and most of his possessions. He became obsessed with his wife, even wishing she were dead so he could stop thinking about her. Can you see his battle to reclaim his attention? He could not imagine having it back as long as she was alive.

This is typical of how strongly we can be bound to what our own evolution has marked to jettison. What is on the periphery is bypassed now as we are compressed and pared down for our own re-birth.

This can be a wrenching experience if we are invested in something that is receding. You can see why murder correlates with Eighth House pieces of time. Crimes of passion are an expression of maximum dependence. Terry's life was ripped down the middle because his attention remained on what was departing. Apparently his wife belonged to his past.

Debts belong to the past, too. They are statements of our dependence on something outside ourselves, and they are likely to be called in during this time if we have at all overreached our ability to carry them.

The Eighth House brings us all to terms with our unfinished business. One member of President Nixon's staff was talking about the Eighth House period of his life when he described going through the Watergate years.

"Watergate totally derailed my life. I had a profession. Now I'm disbarred from practicing law. It gave the coup de grace to my marriage ... and it pretty well stripped me of all my money."

That stripping-down would have happened in some form or other, no matter what this man was doing at the time. It so happens he was in the White House.

Time played a big part in that national crisis. Richard Nixon, himself, was processing the Eighth House during the Watergate years. He entered the Eighth in March of 1972, and the Watergate break-in occurred just three months later. From the Senate hearings and investigation right on through his resignation in August of 1974, President Nixon was confronting his own issues of dominance and control. Mr. Nixon completed his education in *power* just twenty-eight days after lifting off from the White House lawn, pretty much stripped to the bone.

Whether releasing 'the old' means letting go of attitudes or physical belongings, part of our attention is surely on what is departing, and loss is a common symptom of the Eighth House process.

People born to experience the ownership of physical things are likely to receive their losses that way, too, and with four planets processing *havingness* in his Second House, Julian is one of these people. Both he and his wife had good jobs. They were accumulating money, and they had acquired a boat, some property and a vacation home. But as he entered his Eighth House, the company Julian worked for suffered financial difficulties, and some of his staff was let go. Foregoing the open-door policy he valued as a boss, he began retreating into his office and closing the door behind him, recreating the shrinking, Eighth-House space.

At the same time, his wife's job became less secure, and they sold the boat and the land to cut back on expenses. Then brush fires swept through their neighborhood threatening their home, and a neighbor called Julian at work, offering to fetch a few things before he evacuated. Asking what he should rescue, Julian had half an hour to think about it. "In that moment I realized nothing material is important. I couldn't think of anything worth saving," he said.

You can almost hear a latch release the past like a caboose being left behind. Julian's house was spared, but sometimes I wonder what would have happened if they had tried to retrieve their belongings.

Dependencies are power invested in things which are no longer appropriate to our growth, though of course, not everything is inappropriate. Those things in resonance with who we are now fuse during this compression inward, and whether this time involves a stripping-down or a fusion-with is a function of our own process.

If you have planetary energies in this part of your field — which means at about two o'clock in the sky when you were born — they enter into the process, too, and we will talk more about integrating planets later. I have Saturn there, and here is one of my Eighth House threads. At that time I was starting to realize what this cycle looks like. I knew at some point I would study history to see if I could recognize these conditions in our cultural flow, too, but I had never read any history, so this seemed to me like a chore I should leave to my old age when I would have plenty of time.

Yet, while in the Eighth House I happened across a series of books which condense the past into hundred-year segments, and I began flipping through one of them. Soon I had read the whole book and returned to the library for another. After a few round trips, I realized I was coming up on that Saturn — which precipitates and puts a linear form on things. Typically Saturn's quality induces us to acknowledge events and consign them to the past — history. While I was fusing with it, I was able to get a general overview of six thousand years in just a few short months. That opportunity would not happen again for another twenty-seven years.

It is said that planetary energies in the Eighth House have the potential to transform us, and now we know why. We are undergoing a transformation when we integrate them. The realization that this cycle matches the way historians describe history certainly changed me. It renewed my confidence in this research by confirming again that evolution follows a generic sequence, in both our individual and collective experience.

I might point out here it is important to take yourself as the first reference for everything, not your birthprint. What if your birth data is wrong? Your inner voice is already synchronized with your correct birth moment and is in tune with your integration of these concepts. This cycle only validates what we already hear inside. That is all, but that can also be a lot. Once it was clear to me I was approaching Saturn, I knew the motivation to understand history would not be this strong again for a long time. So I took six months to read only that, and I accomplished a lot.

We can deepen our awareness by seeking out the subtleties of our reactions to these qualities. We can be our own teachers. In addition to revealing the conditions of time as separate from who we are, this cycle validates our intuition. Once we realize we are living inside a process, we can take the advice of our inner voice as our guide through life and remain in the present.

THE NINTH HOUSE

Located almost overhead and just to the right, the Ninth House is an expanding space.

A term for a quality needs to cover all of its possibilities, and yet be specific, and I am not completely happy with this one. Each House seems to me like stepping into a chamber with a particular vibration, and *expansion* works for the Ninth House, but I am looking for a better word to describe what happens in this part of life.

This characteristic calls us outward through travel, discovery and education. It increases our connectedness through networks like the Internet. It informs storytelling, publishing, broadcasting, advertising and global communication.

From this condition we interpret paradigms. It holds systems of thought such as philosophy and religion, bodies of knowledge like the legal system and sports. It relates us to the larger social whole.

After an Eighth House collapse, in the Ninth we expand to the far horizons as if we were standing on top of giant sheet of latex being pulled outward in all directions. If the Eighth House has been an especially heavy period, the Ninth can be a welcome release. After his showdown with power during the Watergate years, Richard Nixon was pardoned just two days after entering this space. Whatever had been reconciled as belonging with him and not in his past is what Mr. Nixon took with him when he moved on to his Ninth House.

We manifest this condition in transportation and trade. It is telecommunications, marketing, and somehow music. It increases our connection through exposure to 'the more.'

I got my teaching certificate and moved 5,000 miles away to teach sixth grade in Hawaii while I was in my Ninth House the first time around. Both teaching and moving physically outward express this mode.

So does publishing. I am in the Ninth again as I write this book, and time delivered me right to it. In an effort to downsize, the university where I was working offered incentives to people who would take a lump sum of money to leave. My position there became shaky while I was in my Eighth House, and I know a setup when I see one. I was out of there with enough money to live on and write for six months, and that transition was as easy as getting off an escalator.

Information dissemination is natural in this quality. After a career in the movies as a child star, Shirley Temple hosted a television series built around storytelling while in her Ninth House, though it faded after she left this part of her pattern. If we do not have planets in a House, we are not usually focused on its idea. Our experience of it often dims after we gather from it what we will, as the Progressing Moon moves on.

While in his Ninth House, Kenneth won a seat in the United States Senate. Thomas Jefferson was elected to the Virginia House of Burgesses, and Abraham Lincoln made his bid for election to the Senate against Stephen A. Douglas. All of them were drawn to the Ninth House form of our legal system.

Though she had no training in marketing, Janet took a job in advertising in this House. "I was sent to that company by a temporary employment agency. That was my first assignment and the company asked me to stay. I learned a lot about broadcasting." Janet did not know she was processing this quality, and while she could have been assigned to work anywhere, it wasn't she who chose a firm whose business is information dissemination. The employment agency did. How does *that* work.

As twin experiences of *expansion* — internally on the one hand and externally on the other — the Ninth House is both learning and teaching. We expand inside as we learn, and we extend that outside if we teach.

Ruth emerged from a divorce in her Eighth House to become a teacher while moving through her Ninth. Ruby took instruction to join the Catholic Church. Portia met an Indian Master and was initiated through an Eastern practice. And for the duration of this energy, Paula took a two-year series of seminars from a company promoting itself as an educational system.

Education is a frequent experience of *expansion*, but the Ninth House student is not learning the basics as one in the Third House is. Astrologers refer to the Ninth House as *higher* education because this condition permeates us with a *system* of thought, not just the facts.

But expansion can also mean going outdoors. Sometimes it increases our contact with the natural world, and people who carry a lot of this energy might be park rangers, on the ski patrol, or tour guides. The Sun was here when Jacques Cousteau was born. Others with energy here might be foreign correspondents, broadcasters, orators or storytellers. Or they may be people who hold systems of thought as a profession such as pastors, attorneys, and ministers of state. Broadcaster Hugh Downs was born with the Moon in this part of his sky. Orator William Jennings Bryan has energy here, and so does Rev. Billy Graham.

Giving out is the Ninth House mode. Like all qualities, sometimes it has a literal translation. Antonia started a business while processing this energy, and when I asked what kind she replied, "We sell gift baskets." I have a hard time containing myself when I hear things like that.

Both giving and receiving expand us, but we can feel the benevolence of giving any time we choose. Having completed the Eighth, what we have to give in the Ninth is who we have become. We experience this through the very process of going back out into the world where we are exposed to new information after a period of intense reformation. Whether we disseminate data or become informed ourselves, we gather what is appropriate to our growth now through some larger paradigm.

It is important to know that trying to guess what we will do later is a bit like a six-year old trying to guess what she will do when she is thirty-five. Your inner voice knows what to do, but it speaks in real time, and since this is a constantly updating process, what is appropriate changes. We cannot foresee what experiences will accumulate between now and the future, and of course the choices we make along the way matter. So while time has control of what develops when, we say how sharp the picture will be by steering our attention along the way.

Since our birth pattern has already been printed, what we gain from processing it is depth. Though we may be temporarily invested in some part of ourselves that will eventually be stripped off, in the long run we can only become more of who we already are. We integrate the imprint of our star system and think that is the way life goes. It does, but what would happen if we were born on a planet with two Moons? Or two Suns?

THE TENTH HOUSE

Having recently completed the difficult Eighth House plunge to the bottom line, all that seems important by now is a little recognition, and of course that is the Tenth House.

From the partition overhead and just to the left, we experience *acknowledgement.* Like water vapor condensing to snow, through this quality we crystalize our observations and string them out behind us as history. In the Tenth House we define things.

In this condition we seem to perceive from a tall vantage point. From here we see from high to low, so we comprehend in a vertical way ideas like hierarchy, administration and achievement.

From this perspective we can develop stewardship. This is the tallest observation post, and processing it is like going over the top of a ferris wheel. From here we can observe and validate what is within our domain, confirm and define it, and we experience that as personal responsibility.

In the world this condition manifests retainers, boundaries and borders. It forms structures that protect interior spaces such as architecture, walls, bones and crystals. So it is the house for the home, the cell wall for the cell — and in us, it is responsibility for the indwelling Self. We are as big as our sense of responsibility can hold.

This condition translates to material structures like houses, and Peter bought a house in this part of his life. But if we are not attending to its physical manifestation, the Tenth House will ring acknowledgement.

Portia had been in a long period of internal growth when she entered this House, and after a painful struggle to find work as an actress, she was able to see her situation. "For the first time I refused an audition. In the past I would have taken anything offered, but now I see I am the only one responsible for me. No one else is going to take care of my interests." Why couldn't she see that before? Right timing. Recognition is a Tenth House experience.

Olivia had spent much of her life supporting other people's progress; as she approached her Tenth House, she was assisting the director of a school. Though she had no administrative training and was relatively new in that position, however, she was asked to fill in for her boss as director in his absence. Her success at keeping things running smoothly was part of her Tenth House experience. She was acknowledged for doing well and recognized that she, too, had the capacity to be in charge.

In this energy we develop a kind of parental oversight, but we get an education moving through it even if we are children. Claudia's step-father had been sexually assaulting her for several years, and she is still dealing with the effects of incest. But she was just eleven years old and still a child when she moved into her Tenth House and acquired the personal authority to refuse him for the first time. Folding her arms over her chest she said "No," and he did not enter her space again. Recalling that time, Claudia used a pristinely Tenth House phrase to describe it. "That's when I developed personal boundaries," she said.

Since the Tenth House offers the highest perspective, from here we can see, but we can also *be* seen. This time often brings some kind of public recognition, and whatever we have had our attention on over the years we bring with us into this space. After working against repression within the labor-based Solidarity movement in Poland, Lech Walesa became that nation's first elected President while processing his Tenth House.

As the quality that defines us in the public hemisphere, reputation also descends from here.

Franklin Roosevelt and Bill Clinton were in the Tenth when they were first elected to public office. Abraham Lincoln became President from his Tenth. So did John Adams, Theodore Roosevelt and Calvin Coolidge. Winston Churchill became Prime Minister of England from this frequency, and Thomas Jefferson and William McKinley were processing this concept when they were elected, as was Harry Truman when he inherited the Presidency from FDR. So why aren't all Presidents dealing with this quality when we elect them? They have their own issues, and so does the United States. A President may serve a period in which the nation is purging its past, and the people choose leaders who match their collective need. History is playing a drama of its own, but that's another story.

The Tenth House delivers some form of recognition whether we like it or not, and a person on the run and trying to remain anonymous indeed may not. After almost twenty years in hiding after World War II, Nazi Adolf Eichmann was recognized in Argentina while in his Tenth House. He was taken immediately to Israel, found guilty in a public trial, and hanged as a war criminal before he got to his Eleventh.

People born with planetary energy directly overhead live permanently in a Tenth House kind of consciousness. Hierarchy and achievement are enduring experiences for them. Sometimes described as having the best résumé in government, George Bush is one of these people. He was born when the Sun was overhead. Bill Clinton has two planets here.

As the rest of us integrate this part of the pattern, however, people like entertainers may simply get hot. Their public exposure is peaking. Shirley Temple's breakthrough movie came in her Tenth House, though she was barely six years old at the time. Her run as a child star lasted as long it took her to process the rest of the upper hemisphere, the public part of her life. Her career in movies ended when she entered the lower hemisphere and began processing the personal qualities while in her teens.

Though he was only ten years old, Montgomery Clift was chosen for a part in a Broadway play in his Tenth House. Gregory Peck received his Oscar here, and Donald Trump became a public icon when *The Art of the Deal* was published. Why do public figures peak for a few years, then seem to fade? Our lives adhere to a cosmic schedule, and questions like these have answers in time.

You might feel really on top of things in your Tenth House, and some people choose this time to get married. In the most public wedding of the century, Princess Diana became part of the royal family in this part of her pattern, and the ceremony was the most widely telecast event of our time. What about Prince Charles? This has not been a happy marriage, and he was doing something completely different in those years, which we will look at later on.

The vertical orientation of the Tenth House produces the hierarchy we manifest in organizations. Directorship is a form of seeing from high to low, and to define and be responsible for a situation is what bosses do. Bosses are built to be bosses, though most people are not. This consciousness is necessary to the whole, but it is no more valuable than any of the others. It is a way for bosses, and everyone else, to experience themselves.

In their role to provide safety, to take care of, and to be responsible, fathers carry this archetype. It is their job to furnish the same kind of safety for an interior space that architecture provides for a home. Why do men build houses? Why are fathers concerned with developing responsibility in their children? Why do men emphasize achievement? They have a special resonance with this vertical quality of time.

Though men bear Tenth House awareness, women of course carry it, too, and a certain percentage of women are born with an accent here that makes directing their own lives important to them. Women with this configuration are developing responsibility for themselves, so there may not be room in their lives for the take-care role men play in traditional relationships. Yet while one gender is dominant in each of us, this is a special moment in history when we are all acquiring a more global point of view. We are claiming the lessons of both genders in order to experience our humanity. While women are learning to become more responsible, which some of them experience in careers, men are becoming more inclusive, which makes them more conscious of family and self perception.

Tenth House consciousness is a kind of hyperspace from which we have the ability to see ourselves and to witness our own actions. By gaining perspective, we are taller than our personalities. From here we can see how we operate in the world.

Acknowledgement enables us to recognize who we are and mature as cosmic Beings.

A CLOCK WITH A GRAPHICAL INTERFACE

Sometimes I lie awake at night trying to bend my mind around how this works. I still find it hard to envision just what an astrological chart really is, and where I am in it. So far we have studied time from a flat piece of paper, but I want to see the solar system from space, with a fast-forward and reverse in time, and a zoom to any location.

We should have a start-up screen on our computers that will bring us in from beyond Pluto to an Earth rotating in real time — one that lands us at the location of our choice, then loops down into our desktops and turns our point of view to look back out from where we sit.

When we move, we could change our landing site. When we want to enter another historical period, we could. If we wanted to step into a friend's pattern, we could that, too.

Change has a topography, and a clock like this would help us understand it.

THE ELEVENTH HOUSE

The Eleventh House is *truth*. That is a pretty imposing concept, but we can use a simple definition for it. *Truth is the experience of what is.* Its content is different for everyone.

This quality comes from the second partition overhead to the left. It is whole all at once, in the moment, and this condition resonates with electricity, spark, chi, charisma, intuition and insight. AHA!s are little truths breaking through.

This quality accesses change itself. If the space does not allow for change, *truth* can shatter an enclosure. It will crack crystallized form. This condition prompts us to break any definition that restrains our independence. *Truth* requires the freedom to adjust to time.

This quality also tunes to the human mind. We consider freedom of conscience the standard for basic human rights. We are built to think for ourselves, and governments that punish citizens for what they think are the pariahs of the world.

Since the qualities of time keep changing, *truth* is also a continuing experience of uniqueness. It activates our autonomy as every instant takes its place at the end of a single mutating message: we are not time either. Someone is experiencing the change.

Having assumed self responsibility in the Tenth House, in the Eleventh we shift from recognition to the actual *experience* of something. Here Tenth House hierarchies are suddenly cast off for more egalitarian modes. In this condition we relate to other people as if they were sovereign unto themselves as well. The vertical Tenth House space turns lateral now for the inclusion of like minds, and we share this kind of space with equals. In the Eleventh, we spend time with peers — others like us.

When he reached his Eleventh House, Matthew capped a rewarding career as a surgeon by trading the operating room for service on a medical peer review board. People leading focused professional lives like this seem to look sideways now for others in their space. Matthew spent his Eleventh House steeped in the issues of physicians. And he was more often now in their company.

After attaining a major career goal at the university where she taught, in her Eleventh House Randy began spending more time golfing with her colleagues. Enjoying the company of friends like that is a common Eleventh House experience.

Randy and I are friends. We grew up in the same neighborhood and have known each other since we were three years old. But in all those years, she never visited me — until she reached her Eleventh House. Then she called to say she would like to come to California to spend a few days hanging around. I did not launch into giving my opinion of why.

Because it responds to change, the Eleventh House cuts us loose. Yet for some people that can be uncomfortable. Autonomy can be quite unfamiliar. "I felt like an alien, like I must be from a different planet," was Ellen's reaction to it. People who identify strongly with the past sometimes feel like this.

Jay was uncomfortable here, too, but for another reason. After years as a teacher, he took a personal development class in his Eleventh House and uncovered a reluctance to form friendships. More at home in the teacher's position of authority, he found relationships based on equality difficult. Though it was about friendship, this was not an enjoyable time for him either.

Since the Eleventh House alludes to freedom, this part of the sky also associates with free-lancing, working at temporary jobs, and running your own business. Time is the commodity here, and being in charge of your own time is a major component of this condition. Brenda became a free-lance Art Director in this House.

Though we do not have his exact birth time, Abraham Lincoln probably signed the Emancipation Proclamation while processing freedom himself.

The Eleventh House was especially strong when Adrienne was born. There were two planets here at the time, and she envisions some day running her own business. Her initial experience of that materialized when she processed this House for the first time in her twenties. "I've been hired to run a small company. I work for a shoe designer and I'm having the time of my life," she said as she called to report the good news. Entrepreneurs are people in charge of their own time who use their autonomy to create a living.

Inger recalls this detached mode as the happiest time in her life, too. "Things just seemed to move right along. I went out more, I laughed a lot and I made a lot of friends." Laughter itself is an experience of *truth*. We laugh when we are surprised by a truth we didn't expect, and this condition even prompts some people to express taboos. Comedians George Carlin and Lenny Bruce have planets in the Eleventh House. Its breakaway characteristic makes for rebels of all kinds.

In its delivery of an ever-changing spark of mental energy, this quality produces independent thinkers ranging from comedians and inventors to revolutionaries and outlaws. It prods people like Fidel Castro, John Dillinger and political activist Rennie Davis to test the confining rules of governments. It kindles brilliant minds like Marconi and Thomas Edison to think outside of the way things have already been done. It ignites enthusiasm for taking charge of one's own life. And because it sparks an interest in how time works, it generates excitement about astrology.

Because of a different and much bigger cycle, our new civilization will take shape inside of this condition. As we incorporate its frequency, *truth* and the freedom to operate in real time will be empowering individuals everywhere for the next two millennia. Independence is already on the rise all over the world, and the democracy we see pushing up through repressive regimes is our collective experience of the autonomy this quality delivers. *Truth* will become the force behind healing, the highest standard of conduct, and the condition that sets us free to become thinking human beings. In the next stage of our evolution we are capable of waking up to our human potential — maybe even having the time of our lives.

The New Civilization

The Earth itself processes the same conditions that we experience as individuals through the Progressing Moon. It, too, moves through these qualities, but backwards in a very slow cycle of change. It so happens that due to a megacycle astronomers call The Great Year, the whole planet is entering an Eleventh House condition.

The Earth *precesses* — it wobbles on its axis like a spinning top — making one complete wobble every 26,000 years. This rotates the Earth's orientation to its orbit around the Sun, like a top rolling slowly through a circle as it spins and leans toward the floor.

Everyone on the planet responds to this cycle, but it moves so slowly we only notice it when it carries us all into a new condition. That generates immense turbulence as the culture moves from one idea to another. At these times, civilization begins to do something different, and this is where the idea of a 'new age' comes from.

Our transition from one quality to the next takes decades, perhaps centuries, so it is hard to pinpoint just when we cross into a new condition. But we will know its arrival by the appearance of that condition's characteristics all over the globe, and the next one is due now.

This largest level of change has certainly been driving the upheavals rolling through the twentieth century. Rather than energizing a communal space — which for the past 2,000 years in the West has brought us such forms as monastic life, feudalism, communism and the communal medium of television — the new condition brings independence, freedom, intuition and democracy as a form of government. The hypnotic wavelike frequency of the past is breaking up in a spiky, jolting, electric current, which at this point is the driving force behind out development of computers.

The new frequency localizes in individuals, not groups. It breaks free of mass mind and unplugs from sameness. It promotes independence and self actualization. It supports originality and innovation. If belief filled the sails of our ships in the past, we are adding *truth* as a compass now. Our planet is carrying us into a condition that empowers singular expressions of living time: unique individuals. We are lucky enough to be alive during *this* big change. It is happening to us.

Busting everything from bureaucracies to crystallized thinking, the new energy encourages breaking rank to keep individual synchrony with the natural time of our star system. It cuts us loose into *timing* rather than the kind of time we call history. It abandons the calendar for the pacemaker. It sparks intuition rather than belief and selects creative mind over accumulated fact. So to some degree we are even losing our memories.

But the most obvious sign this change is happening is the global rise of democracy. Empowering individuals makes local governments stronger than federal ones, so inside of large political confederations we get crusades for secession and movements for more national autonomy, like the breakup of the former Soviet Union. This can be a difficult transition, but a people's need to localize as a nation is inevitable now. Many are struggling for self determination, and Chechnya, the Kurds, South Africa, Quebec, Australia, and even Hawaii come to mind. Our resistance to these movements comes from a shared history of 'sameness.' But autonomy is a natural state in the new civilization, and we will have to make room for our local differences.

Though the habits of culture run deep, mapping to any new frequency brings on evolution, and over the last forty years the civil rights movement, the free speech movement, the human potential movement and the global rise of democracy all carry the mark of freedom and respect for the individual — the Eleventh House signature.

As the Age of Faith begins to blur, we experience our new context by telling the truth — individually, one by one — and what cannot hold the truth breaks. Relationships that cannot tell the truth break. Governments that lie, break. And ossified bureaucratic forms which do not serve people break, as individuals, institutions and cultures rip free of their moorings in history.

While telling the truth promotes autonomy, it also opens the heart and resonates with the centerpoint consciousness there. That activates our holograms, and this is why the ancient discipline of time flowers in Eleventh House conditions. It is Earth's precession that is initiating the concept of living 'in real time.' The solar system *is* real time.

As this condition allocates more and more responsibility to the individual, we begin to forsake follow-the-leader. The hierarchal forms are receding, and they are not going to return. The bureaucratic structures that assign bosses responsibility for workers will continue to downsize, and this has big implications for how we make a living. The future supports self actualization, so if you are appropriately cast in what you do, time will promote your creation of that. But having a job is on the way out. Being what we already are must support us from here on. Though it takes courage to assume responsibility for what used to be provided by institutions, we are built to make this change. Human ingenuity is the next great experiment.

In the old civilization, the qualities of time were used to predict the future, and the effects of our solar system were a source of superstition. Do you know what that word really means? Superstition is *an irrational belief in the ominous significance of a thing.* Yet we are aware of time now through experience, not through belief, and at some point we will all know we are simply processing a pattern that shapes our growth as Beings.

The past is starting to look p-r-e-t-t-y unconscious as the old civilization in which we were willing to follow leaders into mutual destruction begins to fade. World War I was close to a family squabble that wiped out millions of people. World War II was played out through the minds of major egomaniacs. And during the Cold War, we had to think hard about whether or not to blow up the Earth. But we did not blow ourselves up, and we are waking up from what seems to be a very disturbing dream. The old game of be-like-me-or-else does not work any more.

When I was in my twenties I read about great Beings and their quests for understanding, and I thought if I were very lucky I could have a life like that in some far distant future. I re-read one of those books recently and realized I am having that life now. Our development as Beings has become an urgent priority, and the push to spiritual enlightenment does not seem to be the private domain of budding Masters any more. A lot of regular people feel something is happening as Earth's Great Year induces us to morph to the condition of *truth.* First we told the truth on Dr. Freud's couch, then to psychoanalysts, then in encounter groups, then in various psychotherapies, then to friends and in support groups of people with similar experiences. Most recently we have carried this conversation onto talk shows. At present, truth-telling is fueling the comedy clubs and cable channels through which laughter is ushering us into the habit of telling it like it is.

Time has given us the job of lightening up. As we step into our new civilization, angels could look down and watch giggling erupt in history. The *big* Age of Enlightenment is on its way, and from space, we ourselves can see that the lights are on. Somebody must be home now.

THE TWELFTH HOUSE

We used to think the universe is constant. With the tools we had it looked pretty much the same all the time, and the Steady State theory was still taught when I was in school. But if you look at pictures of galaxies and nebulae, they look like spinning tops and explosions, and it turns out the universe is a wild place. It is just happening in slow motion.

Though it may seem as if nothing is going on in our lives, either, we are happening in slow motion, too. We can see our process by taking a longer view. With a bigger picture, we can see life change.

We are in a new game now, one in which the competition we have come to expect does not apply. There is no measure for who is ahead or behind when each of us carries a unique set of conditions. In time, there is only doing our best, and success at this level depends on fulfilling who we already are. No one else can contribute your part. No one can perform your function better than you. You are the *only* person, in fact, who can measure your mastery of life, and in the Twelfth House we conduct our own internal review.

Descending into the horizon, from the last partition at the left we experience the finely tuned frequency we associate with ideals.

Here we discern universals, the values that endure beyond all the circumstances. The Twelfth House offers an experience of *oneness*.

We might call this condition love. That term, however, does not fully describe some of the Twelfth House traits. Love is the name we give to the feeling of being complete, which we sometimes feel in the presence of someone else. But as a consciousness, completion is the acceptance of all there is. To come to completion ourselves, we undergo a process of re-evaluation, and a period of retreat is the Twelfth House mode.

Just by living on this planet we express separation. But the Twelfth House frequency tunes us away from our identification with a body and personality and into the universal space. This vulnerable state receives all the others into itself: nothing is excluded from *oneness*. Boundaries undergo a dissolution now, and that can feel like we are 'losing it.'

In a process similar to the Fourth House one, the Twelfth House 'wholeizes.' But here the unifying principle does not shape a personal definition; rather, it releases us into the greater unification of soul, where we surrender through faith, belief and hope.

This is the largest space of them all, and we enter it through forgiveness, meditation, imagination, and wonder. It inspires seekers, monks and mystics, who sometimes experience it as rapture. We know it as ethics and morals, and most often as understanding and 'meaning.'

Because of the sensitivity of this condition, we withdraw from daily life to obtain the stillness and safety we need to enter this period of rest. Monks retire to mountaintops, nuns to cloisters, and ascetics into the deep forest to flow this transcendent space. My friend Annie spent Twelfth House time in an ashram.

In communion with the big picture all the time, people born with planets here are cosmologists, imagineers and spiritual seekers. The teacher Paramahansa Yogananda was born with the Moon hanging low in this sky, and I know a designer for Disney who has his Sun in the Twelfth House. Visionaries of all kinds live here.

But modern life does not mold easily to a withdrawal from routine, so amid the clamor this can be a difficult phase to handle. The Twelfth House is a time to seek sanctuary, to give and receive understanding, and to review the purpose of life. Through this condition, we compare ourselves to the ideal.

Here we are de-focused as we are when we sleep. But since focus is the quality which projects and vitalizes the body, we are physically vulnerable in this condition. Weakness can be one of its symptoms. Physical life may seem heavy enough now to inspire escape through disappearance, drugs or alcohol.

We expect life to be focused on personal concerns, however, so abandoning our individual identity for an immersion in spirit can be disturbing. Dissolution can feel like losing a grip on reality, and we could mistakenly assume that surpassing our personal point of view is a crisis if we do not realize that transcendence is built into the system, too. A period of retreat is natural.

Whatever we have done in the previous cycle begins to fall away as understanding it all now becomes a priority. Either we retire from life or it retires from us, and the focus on daily routine dissipates. In this space we contemplate the unifying qualities which give life real meaning like compassion, acceptance and love. Removal into privacy is the orthodox way of doing that, so thinkers may retreat into solitude, and those working to bring spiritual understanding into everyday life might even translate this to spending some of their Twelfth House time in jail. Seekers of unification are people like Albert Einstein, Mohandas Gandhi, and Nelson Mandella.

Those who are not grounded in material reality, however, might feel this added dissociation as flying a bit too far out and a little too close to schizophrenia. This ethereal space can even nudge a person to seek psychiatric help or into confinement in a mental hospital. If we find here that our life has no meaning, we feel depressed; and if we have no hope we may want to die. We might face how much of both we have while we process this part of life.

83

In general we experience the Twelfth House as *pattern dissolve*, a period when the forward motion of life seems to dwindle. Though he was just fourteen years old, Mike was expelled from school in this House, and he never went back. Instead he joined a theater troupe and began creating illusion, his expression of the unmanifest world. His old life faded forever, and he went on to create an entirely new persona as an actor.

Leaving a way of life behind like that is typical of this part of the pattern. The first time Fran slipped into this deep space, she was only two years old, yet even at that age her life disintegrated. Her parents were divorcing. Twenty-seven years later, she went through the same dissolution again. After leading a sophisticated existence attending the symphony and dining in French restaurants with her companion, the two of them broke up when she entered the Twelfth House this time. For a year she withdrew into her apartment and saw almost no one except a psychiatrist, who, in Twelfth House fashion, took her through a process of understanding. "The meaning had gone out of my life," she said. In fact, she was discovering meaning by its absence. The subject of meaning had come *into* her life.

This is a good time to mention something intriguing about relationships. The people we choose to be with often reflect the energy we are processing at the time. When Fran met her partner she was in her Tenth House, and he had strong Tenth House energy. Had they been a good match for the long run, they might have passed through this period of re-evaluation. But relationships that are pasted together or serve just a local part of our growth do not survive this dissolution, and their time passes. Carl, for instance, got married when he integrated his Tenth House. But there was a lot of conflict between him and his wife, and when he moved into his Twelfth, they divorced. Jim and Lorraine got engaged while they were both in the Eleventh, but broke it off in the Twelfth. We defer to timeless values here through a period of re-evaluation.

Though a less common time for pairing up, when marriage is a Twelfth House event, it is probably undertaken with regard to some greater set of principles. Prince Charles married Lady Diana from his Twelfth House. He has said it was his consideration for royal duties and his obligation to provide heirs to the crown that induced him to marry when he did. Bowing to pressure from his parents, he was deferring to the greater need while tuned to this frequency.

Though this marriage has come undone, I have also encountered good marriages made at this time. Perhaps these are people who relate to each other primarily as souls. Even if these partnerships do not work out, maybe they are especially karmic matches. Whenever a marriage is made, or whenever any significant event occurs for that matter, it reflects our evolutionary process somehow.

As part of the unmanifest spirit world, sleep also associates with this quality. Renata is a sensational example of that. As she progressed through her Twelfth House, this woman suddenly began falling asleep in public. At any hour of the day she could go unconscious, and did, and here she began suffering from narcolepsy. This sudden and uncontrollable need for sleep was acquired in the de-focused space that dissolves us into the unmanifest part of the spectrum. It induced Renata right into a sleep state.

Since it rejects nothing, the Twelfth House condition has no capacity for resistance, and acceptance is one of its issues. People born with planets in this part of the sky are sensitive to whether others are accepted, as well. As a political activist, John used this period to challenge a city policy of denying access to the library to a particular group of people. For his civil disobedience, he was arrested and sent to jail. While processing acceptance, he was especially aware that some people were being left out, and he wanted to influence the values of the community.

Loren was also concerned with community values in her Twelfth House, and she had a similar experience. Because it affected her neighborhood, she became enmeshed in a law suit and fought hard, she said, 'because of the principle of the thing.'

Now that we know this is a period in everyone's life and that contemplation is not reserved for special people, maybe someone will design the Twelfth House Inn in the deep woods where no one speaks, everyone attends alone, and a ritual space is provided for reflection. As a service to the spiritually frazzled, perhaps we could check into a room with a bed and a robe and be received into a group of chanting monks who would hold the proper decorum and act as guides for people who are integrating the idea of *oneness*.

We have internalized our planet's participation in time as one holographic reality, and this is the last of its twelve partitions. These twelve qualities describe how human beings hold the cycle of change. We experience it as a sequence of ideas we process inside ourselves.

Though we have not yet learned how this works, time is our new education, and through this cycle we actually experience its characteristics.

The Passing Civilization

Since civilization processes these conditions, too, they form a giant cycle in history. We have been in the condition we are completing now for 2,000 years, and after so long inside the same idea, we naturally assume that this one is all there is.

But our personal experience of time uncovers its cyclic nature. Simply by living, we find that a regular sequence of conditions is built into being here — and that no one of them lasts forever.

The entire planet has been receiving instruction about *oneness* for twenty centuries now. To manifest this condition's retreat into spirit, in the West we established The Church as a dominant force. About half way through this period, it flowered as we gushed our spiritual aspirations into the interiors of gothic cathedrals. About a thousand years ago, too, we pushed out in Viking boats across the globe from east to west, and Norsemen met their Asian counterparts for the very first time in North America, be it again a bloody calling card. Nevertheless, there we drew the first thin human circle around the entire planet that set us up for an experience of *oneness* planet-wide at the end.

For these long centuries, too, we have probably been especially susceptible to sickness and plague. The classic Twelfth House state is a vulnerable one, and our physical weakness may well fade into the past as Earth is released from this period of confinement. Our history of feeling defenseless may be playing its way through our psyche as we take a final stand against AIDS.

In this civilization's closing moments, we would make some concluding statement about living together in a larger common reality without boundaries, and we have already done so. Without realizing it, in one grand experience which includes us all, we have seen ourselves whole from space. Our *oneness* has already happened.

While we thought we were going to the Moon, in fact the significance of making that trip has not been Moon rocks, but the happening of global Earth. Our astronauts report that gazing back at our planet was a religious experience, a rapture of impersonal unity, and many of them were overwhelmed by a profound sense of love.

Whatever spiritual awareness we have gleaned individually, we have internalized *oneness* collectively as an experience of love for our planet. After a labor two millennia long, we have delivered *oneness* into physical reality. Spaceship Earth has been born in the communal mind, and we have attended the birth.

THE PLANETS

If the twelve Houses are the itinerary of our growth, there are some major points of interest along the way. Earth's siblings were somewhere in the global space around us when we were born, and after having imprinted their positions, we integrate them, too.

Planets occur at special intervals moving out from the Sun, at such predictable points that before we had good telescopes we found the last two by knowing mathematically where the next one should be. Now, here is another fascinating aspect of time. We find that circumference correlates with radial distance — distance around with distance out — and each of the planets conveys one of the twelve conditions of the spherical space shrunk onto us from the sky.

So in addition to the two-and-a-half year integration of a House, we get a nugget of its quality in one shot when we process the planet with that characteristic. It could be anywhere in our pattern. Now that the experience of a birthprint can be separated through time, we can verify for ourselves the quality a planet conveys when we process its degree.

Though each planet delivers one of the twelve conditions, the association between planets and Houses is not a straightforward one. A planet's position outward from the Sun does not correlate with the House we might expect — the nearest with the First House, the farthest with the Twelfth. We are one planet short, too, so the picture is incomplete. This makes all the new information coming back from our planetary fly-bys particularly interesting.

Astrologers, for instance, long ago noticed the color blue-green associates with Neptune. Voyager affirmed that Neptune *is* blue-green. Mars associates with the color red, and itself is red. Then there is the delightful case of Uranus, which adds an element of non-conformity to a pattern. Uranus is the only planet to roll around the Sun on its side. We are discovering that the physical properties of planets correlate with our experience of them here on Earth. We are close to having a continuum of information extending from our exploration of a planet as matter through our experience of it as Beings.

If you were born when several planets were in the same part of the sky, in conjunction, you will process them within a few months of each other. This brings on a dynamic period. Because we integrate one degree of our birthprint every month, when several planets are close together, their properties line up for integration. In comparison to the several years we take to integrate a whole House, a planet is a compact bundle of traits, and in this case we would process several different ideas in a short time.

Usually we can feel our approach to a planet from several degrees away, which is several months in time. Its condition will be in sharpest focus as we pass directly over it.

Though we have inherited much of this understanding, there is nothing sacred about these descriptions that our experience cannot revise. It is our turn to interpret time's correspondence with life, and having looked at the characteristics of time in our spherical space — the Houses — here now are short descriptions of the planets that resonate with them.

MARS

Mars carries the First House quality of *will*. Integrating this degree brings a piece of time that projects, and things such as one's personal presentation, the eyes and our attention correlate with our experience of this planet's imprint. Here is an amazing example affirming Mars' delivery of First House characteristics.

Angela's pattern places an emphasis on her First House, and something most unusual happened that related her experience of this House with Mars later on.

Angela was just a baby when she first processed this House, and during that time she lost her right eye to disease. She was immediately given a glass eye replacement, but one that gave her a slightly off-center look. That set her up for a preoccupation with her somewhat cockeyed appearance. She was continually aware of her presentation, which is a classic First House education in *will*.

More than thirty years later, she revisited this situation when she processed Mars in her pattern. Its qualities were emphasized for a few short weeks now, and she chose that specific time in her life to have a new glass eye made. After a series of modifications, and while immersed in this kind of consciousness, she emerged with a new look that now pleased her very much.

Both Mars and the First House brought dramatic experiences with her eyes, the carriers of our attention and the organ that determines the external placement of the *will*.

Eyesight is one way of projecting ourselves, one form of moving outward from where we are, and to separate from prevailing circumstances is another. Prince Charles stated his experience of Mars in this manner — literally, and exactly as he integrated this planet. That month the Prime Minister of England read this message to the House of Commons:

> *"It is announced from Buckingham Palace that, with regret, the Prince and Princess of Wales have decided to separate."*

The word "separate" refers to the Mars capacity. In his own twenty-seven year cycle, Prince Charles was steeped in the idea of going his own way precisely that month, while integrating his Mars.

Gavin made nearly the same interpretation of this planet. Married for four years, when he processed Mars in his pattern he initiated proceedings to divorce.

Because having a body is the Being's way of projecting itself into physical reality, we associate this quality with other kinds of vehicles, too. Taylor expressed her Mars that way. Imprinted from just below the horizon at her left, her Mars not only relates to the First House, as everyone's does, it is in it. That combines the Mars projective quality with more projection. As if launching herself, when she integrated her Mars she took up sailboat racing.

Yet here is quite a different experience of Mars — and a remarkable one, too. After coming down with multiple sclerosis, Louise had been in a wheelchair for six years. While integrating her Mars, however, she began an electric stimulation treatment to re-route the nerve transmissions that were not getting to her muscles. In a dramatic turnaround, she was up and walking again in the space of a week. "I could see I had given up," she said. While taking in the Mars consciousness, she not only found a way to circumvent the impaired nerves so that she could again mobilize her muscles, she re-installed her *will* to recover. She has been walking ever since.

Will is what we use to enter and steer our ship, and astrologers have known for a long time that Mars activates the muscles. They respond to our use of *will*.

You can see how specific these experiences are, yet they all project the qualities of *will*, and they were all brought forth in the Mars degree.

VENUS
The Second House Version

Venus resonates with two parts of the birthprint, so this is an area to sort out. In both cases, integrating it brings a *reflective* kind of space.

We can be reflected by people through relationships in its Seventh House association, but we are also reflected in physical reality by the things we own.

Venus in its Second House mode relates to *havingness*. It brings experiences about sufficiency, value, confidence and self esteem — ideas often represented by money. More deeply, it is the experience of *trust*.

The Second House qualities of Venus were present in Pamela's experience of it. After working many years as a cashier, she managed to cover her expenses and live within her means, but she could not get interested enough in money to plan for her old age.

Then she passed over Venus and inherited $19,000. Making a full-steam effort to learn how to invest her money, within six months she had earned several thousand dollars more. "I can't believe how easy reading about money is now. Suddenly financial magazines make sense," she said. "Where have I been?"

She has been in 'the before.' We cannot make anything happen before its time. Either we are not interested, or forcing an interest does not work. Whether we are aware of it or not, when an energy presents itself, it colors our perception, and somehow our circumstances as well. To process an energy is to *be* interested, and Pamela was able to put her mind to creating some financial stability while passing through this kind of consciousness.

The people for whom money is not a blank page in the themebook of life are most likely born with planets in the Second House, and it is their job to deal with ownership. Though Pamela was not one of these people, she inherited actual dollars, gained a trust in handling her finances, and experienced a sense of confidence as she passed over Venus. Whether she would have developed the interest in finance without inheriting the money we will never know. But her level of confidence would have come up at this time somehow. It is a basic experience of *trust*.

Jack had been elected to the Board of Directors at a Fortune 500 company and was generally giving the other directors a collective headache with his constant pressure to change things. They disagreed about how the company should be run, and he held out against them for two years before they decided to pay him off and get rid of him — exactly as he crossed his Venus. He walked away with many millions of dollars, unaware, I am sure, of time's role in this. Venus resonates with money, illustrating again that life has its own agenda.

It is people born with a Second House emphasis who would make a practice of promoting prosperity consciousness, sometimes implying we can all make a lot of money if we only emulate them. In fact, we cannot emulate them unless we are already built as they are, in which case money is probably not a problem for us either. We pay attention to this subject when we tune to it naturally, and money is a Second House and Venus concern.

Yet, ultimately all we really own is our word. Giving one's word has always been considered a seal on an internal commitment. It is a form of saying that we can be trusted, and Venus also resonates with the voice. In the short time Corrinne was processing this planet, she enrolled in a class entitled *Here's Your Voice*, promoted as a means of developing confidence, a Venus state of mind.

Though a piece of time might make more sense in the light of some other part of the pattern later on, if you look at the concept you are integrating now, you will see it in your life. It's there. If you are passing over Venus, look for havingness.

With computers we can calculate when our private climate of energy changes and lay out the entire cycle of a life. When we look back, the Progressing Moon's cycle of conditions will match our experience, and more than once if we live long enough.

MERCURY

Mercury brings a condition that connects. This quality advances such things as gathering information, reporting, reading, writing, commuting, and the physical connections made by people like mailmen and couriers when they make their deliveries.

As an environment, Mercury seems to link things up. We extend this condition to siblings, neighbors and community, and in the body it makes nerves and dendrites. In general it is *communication*, the Third House idea.

Information is the commodity here. Students live in this kind of space, and when I encountered Mercury I was attending a weekly study group organized to discuss a book. I was only in that group for the few weeks of my pass over this planet, and that short part of my life is also an example of how a planet expresses not only its character, but its orientation in a birthprint.

Mercury in the sky was on the other side of the Earth when I was born, at my back and located about halfway up to my right palm if I were lying feet-to-the-south on the ground. That put it in my Fifth House, where it resonates with creativity. The book was about how to create.

If you can hold these two ideas — a planet and its House position — you are a long way toward understanding your birth pattern and what it means to have something like 'Mercury in the Fifth House.' So try holding one more dimension. At the time of night I was born, the Fifth House looked out on the seasonal section of the Earth's orbit we call Pisces — and we will look at sign energies later. That added Pisces characteristics to this part of my imprint, too, and ideas such as imagination and spiritual values vibrate with the Pisces part of the spectrum. I pulled that book off my shelf to recall what was in it. Though I was not aware at the time of what I was processing, in the front I had written a summary note: "Prayer, imagination, faith, creation." And we think we are in charge.

I checked my printout for the United States to see what we were doing as a country when we integrated Mercury. There is a beautiful example of connection there. While pulling off this degree in 1869, we joined the Union Pacific with the Central Pacific to complete the first transcontinental railroad. That's an actual physical embodiment of *communication*.

Sometimes planetary degrees are hard to locate in our experience as we look back, so don't be discouraged if this is so for you. We are trying to recall a few short weeks from perhaps many years ago, and often we just cannot remember what went on. Mercury is never more than twenty-eight degrees from the Sun, so these two imprint close together in a pattern. When people search for an experience of this planet, it is sometimes outshone in memory by our experience of the Sun. We can be totally unconscious of processing a planet until we have a handle on its quality.

Most of us have no idea why change really occurs, and I like to watch us make up reasons for what we do. I thought I joined that book discussion group because I was invited by someone I liked. Even allowing that as a reason, I stayed because that book was about what I was about.

These illustrations are not presented to convince you or to convert you to a point of view. They are intended to interest you in your own process. You are not your life, nor the conditioning attached to the pattern you carry, but a Being who transcends them both.

THE MOON

Remember when *Be Here Now* was a radical idea? When I grew up, the past was the most popular tense, and there were a few futurists, but the present was a vacant lot.

It turns out that *now* — the present — is a changing reality conditioned by the Moon. That seems exotic, doesn't it.

The Moon's orbit contains only the Earth, and it relates to our planet as no other celestial body does. The Moon's space *includes* ours, and we apparently holograph that relationship by including our experiences to make one whole thing inside ourselves. The Moon holds *self perception*.

The planets are hands on a clock the same as the hands on wall clocks are, but each of them is also a process. Of all the processors, by progression, only the Moon glides through every House and across all the other planetary placements in a birth pattern before we die. Relating to the Fourth House, the Moon carries our perception through the entire birthprint, presenting conditions for our integration as it goes. Our inclusion of its changing qualities generates a sense of Self and molds our evolution as Beings.

After some twenty-seven years, the progressing Moon returns to its original degree, at which time most people undergo some kind of completion, especially women who resonate with the Moon. Who-we-are-to-ourselves-alone is integrated in this part of life, and now the process is to perceive Self and come to terms with our internal sense of home. It seems natural to think of this as the first maturity.

The Moon also relates to mothers. They hold the space of who we are for us until we can assume it for ourselves. That is often when we integrate our original lunar degree.

Veronica had a very difficult relationship with her mother, an alcoholic who made a practice of squelching her with the phrase "Who do you think you are?!" This is a pristinely lunar question. When Veronica was twenty-seven, precisely as she integrated her Moon, her mother died. Life reassigned the lunar question to her now. It must have been time for Veronica to hold that space herself.

For some people, however, perceiving Self means to begin holding a space for another Being, and becoming a mother is a common way for women to process this degree. Bonny had a baby when she was twenty-seven. So did Grace and Sarah. By the inclusion of someone else, motherhood mimics the Earth-Moon relationship — first biologically as the baby grows inside the woman's body, and then psychologically as she runs the home in which the child grows up. I find it interesting that we do not call our planet *Father* Earth. Perhaps if we had no Moon we would.

The perception of who we are through the inclusion of qualities of consciousness is an archetypally female process. You can almost see a little girl pressing the shape of inclusion around her doll as she cradles it in her arms. Women even copy this shape into handbags and purses in emulation of the Moon.

Penny was adopted when she was a baby, and eventually she wanted to find out where she came from to fill the gap in her past. Completing a sense of self fills a lunar need, and after a long search,

Penny's past came together in a lunar time. She found her birth mother while integrating her Moon.

Biographers of the Indian teacher Ramakrishna report that at one point in his life he wished to expand his experience of gender by dressing as a woman. He was processing his Moon at the time.

When Talia processed her Moon, she decided not to marry the man she had been seeing for four years. "He wanted to have children, and I felt as if I were at a crossroads between motherhood and something I didn't know about yet. That's when I started looking for who I am." Breaking up with this man diverted Talia from becoming a mother, but it transposed her process to one of self discovery instead. "That's what my life is about now," she said.

Trained as a designer, Kim got her first good job as she processed her Moon. She was describing her self perception when she referred to being hired. "That was the first job I had working at who *I* thought I was."

But the experience of self can also be a traumatic time. Perhaps a measure of self-loathing came up for these people. Musicians Janis Joplin, Jimi Hendrix and Kurt Cobain all died by their own hand during their Progressing Moon return to the birthprint's original lunar degree.

As a young nation, the first time the United States returned to its lunar degree, evidently we perceived ourselves as bigger than we were. While appraising our internal home, we promptly decided to add more room. We processed our Moon in 1803 and about doubled our size with the Louisiana Purchase.

In our national return to the Moon again in 1940, Superman debuted in a syndicated radio program. Sometimes spectacular archetypes like this show up in planetary degrees. It seems we think of ourselves as champions of truth, justice and the American way. In the Third House, as it is in America's birthprint, the Moon shapes our concept of self within a context of communication — information, community, reading and writing. Clark Kent was a newspaper reporter.

Putting another spin on ourselves as a people who regard free communication as a major part of who we are, when we returned to this degree in 1967 we funded the Public Broadcasting System to support educational television. With appropriate timing, we were integrating our Moon again in the spring of 1995 when we reviewed the entire practice of funding PBS. At the same time, we passed the first bill since 1934 to address communication law.

In a mysterious reverberation of the Superman archetype, that is also when Christopher Reeve, who played Superman, broke his neck in a riding accident. I don't know what to make of that.

We continue to add to how we perceive ourselves and take a second look at who we think we are at about the age of fifty-five. During this pass over his Moon, Jim reduced his surgical practice to half its size to begin a more creative life as an author. Mikhail Gorbachev was elected General Secretary of the Communist Party that year. We could call this pass the second maturity.

All our experiences end up inside our evolving perception of Self, which in turn becomes how we perceive everything else. Inclusion, integration, and Self perception are tied to the Moon.

"Just give me something big to do," one friend of mine pleads to no one in particular. "I can't stand the small stuff any more." She is referring to small stuff like a job. "I need to be something more, I just don't know what it is." In our time, the *doing* does not seem to be a problem — finding out *what* to do, is. Self knows what to do, but it is probably not something already out there. In a time of self actualization, creativity is the driving force, and we will look at that processor next.

THE SUN

Our Sun is thought to be an average star somewhere in the middle of its life. It contains more than ninety-nine percent of the mass in the whole solar system and by far overwhelms the tiny bodies whirling around it. Its exploding prominences struggle against a forceful magnetic field, and the curvature of space that directs every celestial body in our neighborhood is anchored by this dynamic cauldron of creation. The Sun is the centerpoint of our star system, and we replicate that reality, too.

But before we look at a few examples, we should know that in the turn of Age taking us into a new civilization, the Sun plays a major part. The awareness of time developing over the next 2,000 years is anchored by the Sun.

We anchor the experience of time in ourselves through *creativity*. Creative self actualization is our full expression of the changing conditions of time.

We have encounters with that when we process the Sun, and again when we move through the Fifth House, the long version of a solar education.

Circulating vitality in the body, the heart simulates the solar hub. As the figure at the center, royalty is the solar archetype, and the Sun rings truest in physical reality with the noble metal gold.

Solar light contains the whole rainbow of colors, and we express this widest spectrum of energy most simply through our behavior. Beyond that, this consciousness is the vitality behind any creative expression.

When Carolina crossed this part of her pattern she was infused with the creative process. In those few weeks she took a class on mental imaging and learned to mock up the kind of life she wanted to live.

Judy started writing when she integrated this part of her pattern, composing her first performance piece at this time, she said, in order to express who she is. The self actualizing creative energy of the Sun is in that piece.

Though Lorraine had painted for years, she created her first major work when she processed her Sun. "For the first time a piece was really me," she said. "That painting holds a special place in my development as an artist." It is, in fact, an expression of her Being. Solar consciousness *is* being. The Sun doesn't do — it be's.

John was fifty-three as he crossed his Sun, and while you might think he would initiate something creative here, too, instead he sold his multi-million dollar corporation. He had built that business from scratch, and as he considered his creative potential, he must have felt that his company did not embody it any more. He let the business go and has since built another one.

Evelyn was fifteen when she processed her Sun, and that month she was elected an officer of the Student Council. "That was forty years ago, but what I remember about that time was feeling full of myself," she said. Remote as that association is, Evelyn's memory recreates the consciousness whose nature is to illuminate the whole spectrum of who we are.

I had recognized this cycle before I integrated my Sun, so I was keeping notes of my experiences when I passed through its space. They were archetypal as I approached this regal quality one year at Christmas. I received three presents that year: a lamp described on its package as *The Princess Lamp*; two foil-wrapped candies, one with a crown on it and one with a heart on it; and an invitation to a party at a club called *The Palace*. None of the people giving me these presents knew anything about this cycle, yet each of those gifts has royal associations that correlate with the solar energy I was processing. How does that happen?

Victoria chose this moment in life to begin a discipline called Actualism, the stated purpose of which is to uncover the archetypal pattern for expressing our total Being. That is a tidy definition of self actualization.

And what is going on here? Jackie Kennedy was processing her solar degree that day in Dallas when President Kennedy was shot.

As a general source of energy for heating and cooling, the idea of sun power is entering our culture at this time in history for good reason. As the new civilization begins to activate the solar quality in us all, we translate it directly to ideas like solar energy.

We are also the first to attempt heart transplants. And it is our generation that developed the pacemaker to keep artificial time for the heart. Timing and the Sun go together, rendered in the body as the pacemaker and the heart.

For the next 2,000 years, our experience of time's changing conditions will be complemented by self actualization. Our job at this juncture in history is to transpose the old way of life to the new one. We are to raise *doing* to *being* — and every twenty-seven years, being an instrument of creation is a personal experience when we integrate our Sun.

CHIRON

There are many more celestial bodies in our star system than the eleven we will consider. Thousands of asteroids are floating along out there, most of them between Mars and Jupiter, and there are various other bodies scattered around — some of them studied, by the way, by astrologers doing seminal research on their effects.

I believe our time will mark our emergence from a pre-conscious history. Our milestone planetary fly-bys, on the one hand, are matched on the other by a new generation of timekeepers who are restoring our internal relationship with the solar system as well. Our initiation into natural time is expanding our awareness of both physical space and personal development. We have a place in a larger whole, now, and that provides a context for becoming more conscious of ourselves as well as our planet.

Astrologers have been studying Chiron since Charles Kowal detected it from Mt. Palomar in 1977. Orbiting between Saturn and Uranus and originally called an asteroid, then a planetoid, this body is now thought to be the largest known comet nucleus, most likely captured from a reservoir of objects beyond Neptune and Pluto called the Kuiper Disk.

Chiron is huge, about the size of New Hampshire, and it shows Sixth House characteristics. Isolating a body by noticing what comes up when we integrate its degree is a beautiful technique for understanding its qualities, and Chiron seems to correlate with processing — the act itself. As a state of consciousness, we experience that as *choice*.

Choosing keeps the energy flowing. *Choice* is how we process the flow of time through daily life. In the body, choosing maintains our physical health.

We are just beginning to collect information about Chiron, so my files have only a few scant references to encounters with it. But here is some of what we know about it so far.

Bridget has had a lifelong struggle with guilt. "Every time I make a decision I feel guilty if it's not what other people want me to do," she said.

Bridget had just accepted another long-term assignment in a stressful situation as a substitute teacher when she began to process Chiron. "Though I accepted that job, I chose not to continue. Normally I'd blame myself for not being able to do a job, but for some reason making that choice was easy. I didn't feel any guilt at all."

In this very small window of time, upsetting other people became secondary to her, and Bridget was able to end a long string of draining assignments while saturated with Chiron. Making a choice now had more momentum than her fear of disappointing others, which had thrown up resistance to choosing before.

When people describe a piece of time potent with a specific energy, watch the words they use. Bridget used the word *choice* to frame this whole incident. While making choices may be easy for some people, they have not been easy for her, and that changed in this piece of time.

Here is another example of integrating this idea. Whereas Victoria began the discipline of Actualism while crossing her Sun, Carol began this same discipline while assimilating her Chiron.

Though this regimen aims for self actualization, processing is its method, its essence, and she entered into this training in a period brimming with *choice*.

During World War II the United States was integrating Chiron at the very moment we launched our troops into Normandy on D-Day in June of 1944. There were other powerful influences in America's birth pattern that year, but we integrated Chiron exactly that month. The Allies were under General Eisenhower's command, and astrologers have found that leaders acting on our behalf step into the national birthprint. Chiron in America's birthprint associates with projecting, initiating, starting and beginning, and on D-Day the space was offering something like 'process beginning.'

General Eisenhower was having his Second House experience of *trust* and commitment at the time, and this is the idea he would have been working from while waiting for the right weather conditions to launch the largest invasion force in history. With the Progressing Moon as a timer, we can know what personal conditions are involved in decisions like this.

Once we can see the flow of characteristics, we can also see that life's conditions are delivered by time. We did not design the river, we are simply navigating it, and *choice* is our rudder.

The United States processed Chiron again in 1971, the year we began manufacturing and marketing microprocessors on chips. Looking back on our relationship with computers and information since then, in a flipped over version of our experience on D-Day, that certainly looks like 'begin processing' to me.

Since our Being is already in synchrony with change, we do not need to know anything about energy patterns to live our lives. The intuition for what to do, and when, comes from the part of us that is already in touch with changing conditions. But we can become conscious of operating in this dimension and add meaning to what seems to be a random flow of ups and downs if we connect ourselves with nature. All these examples are demonstrations of a life bigger than the one we are leading now. We may soon bypass these smaller vignettes to live in our grander stories.

We are always inside the flow of time, but when our attention snaps into synchrony with its qualities, we can feel it. Synchrony has a rightness to it, even if we are aligning with a difficult process, and we mark these periods as special. So we only have to seek from memory the incidents that have significance to us to see the conditions doled out by the integration of our own birthprint.

While we cannot be out of synchrony, expanding our reality to include time as part of the natural world puts us in a position to make sense of life in a new and bigger way. If an experience is pivotal to you, look to the energy expressed there to expand your understanding. The event will teach you how you have integrated an energy, and that you are indeed choosing your way through time.

EARTH'S FIRST FAMILY PORTRAIT

In 1989 I went to Pasadena to watch the pictures come in from our Neptune fly-by. These first looks at the planets will never happen again, they are historic occasions, and The Planetary Society had organized an event so the public could see the images JPL was receiving from our Voyager spacecraft.

During that day's press briefings and commentary as images were unveiled and projected slowly and dramatically onto giant screens, I heard a rumor that the project manager was thinking about turning Voyager's camera back toward the Sun. After passing Neptune it would be possible to capture the planetary family in one picture if we were to look back over Voyager's shoulder as it sailed on out of the solar system.

To astrologers, "firsts" are significant events, and to me this was an exciting prospect. So during a question period I asked whether that picture would in fact be taken. While the question was dismissed as if it were not very important, I knew if we took that snapshot it would come from the heart of a very special piece of time. Without blurring our focus on the Progressing Moon, I should tell you that I also study the flow of generations through history, and 1989 was a pivot in our cultural development. Having that photo would be a statement of just how sharp a turn we were making in our evolution as a people. It would declare to future generations just what we were thinking about at the very core of our transformation, and we were thinking about belonging to a star system.

The picture was indeed taken. I don't care at all that we can hardly see the inner planets from that distance — that they are blurry and Earth is a tiny fuzzy dot. Future generations will know about the characteristics of time, and in that context, that picture says a lot. It says this is when we knew we belonged to the stars. This is when we first saw ourselves as bigger than even a planet. This is when we gave ourselves the space in which to become a global civilization. This is when the Earth became our body and space became our home, too. This is when we woke up, and looked around to see where we were.

VENUS

The Seventh House Version

Remembering that birth patterns are imprinted spherically, our public development is imprinted from the hemisphere overhead, measured from the right palm circling up across the sky and down again to the left one.

In the section just above the horizon at the right, we register our initial exposure to the world at large. Venus resonates with this part of the sky, the Seventh House area of *reflection*.

Venus is the only planet we associate with two parts of the birthprint, and while it reflects us through material havingness in its Second House correlation, we are also mirrored through relationships, and that is its Seventh House association.

What we see in others — what they return to us — is our own energy, and the chemistry we experience with someone else is our interaction with that person's energy pattern. Some energies absorb. One forms a natural fence. Others project, connect, expand or disperse. So some patterns feel good in the presence of each other, while others do not.

Performing the archetypally female function, Venus is often represented as a woman's hand mirror. Through it our projection into the world bounces back to us and reveals us through the reactions of other people.

Rachel recounts her Venus crossing this way. "I was twenty-one and just starting to make my way in the art world when I fell in love with a fabric designer. He made me feel good about myself as an artist," she said. We usually interpret Venus as being noticed, being seen, being appreciated by someone else — and we often experience it through lovers. This man appreciated Rachel's artistic ability.

While integrating her Venus, Dinah met someone who made a profound impression on her. "I know this man," was her instant response to him. In her small Venusian packet of time, someone she felt was her destined partner appeared. We recognize ourselves in others, and when another reflects the good in us, we want to be with them. Dinah felt she had been waiting all her life for just this person.

The first time she processed Venus, Emily was only five years old. When I inquired whether she could remember anything about September of that year she replied, "Yes, my brother was born. I've always felt in past lives we could have been lovers."

Frances was just seventeen and dating someone she did not like very much when she crossed Venus for the first time. That month she was elected Queen of the high school dance. What she remembers about that event, however, is the boy who was elected King. He asked her out and she realized she could attract someone else. He reflected her in a way her boyfriend did not.

Crossing that Venus again later in life brought her the same sort of response. Having recently taken a position at a large company, her new boss took a special liking to her. "I had forgotten all about that feeling, it was really nice to be noticed again," she said. She felt appreciated once more during a period that reveals us through our reflection in other people.

Steven got married while crossing his Venus. So did Linda, and these are two other examples of the Venus correlation with relationship. But here are two experiences of Venus that are interesting because they do not match the typical scenario, and they are similar to each other.

In both situations, friends died. Arthur was the lead skier in a group when he headed into an avalanche zone. While traversing a slope their party set off a huge slide of snow, and one of Arthur's friends was killed. In the other case, the very wealthy owner of a large company lost three of his colleagues in a business-related helicopter crash as he was integrating this planet. After that event, he said he realized that life is short and that his marriage was not a very good one. The Venus conditioning would put the experience of partnership forward, where brushes with death might underscore its quality. Both of these men soon separated from their wives.

And look at this occurrence. Beverly was in a bad accident as she passed over Venus and plunged headlong through the windshield of her car. She was taken immediately to the hospital, and there she had an out-of-body experience. "I could see myself, but more than that, I had an ecstatic encounter with these tall, beautiful beings. I felt unconditional love coming from them and it was wonderful." Beverly was processing that Venus through her Twelfth House, the dimension of spirit, where the context is one of total acceptance. Her reflection there from these beings was an experience of unconditional love. Amazing.

Other people may be unable to see the energy in your life, but they are not in the loop. You are the only person to experience the conditioning you carry and to feel what chords reverberate inside when specific conditions are activated. Knowing the quality of a piece of time will make it visible to you in your own exceptional way, though probably to you alone.

PLUTO

Life may sail along without special events for quite a while as very few of the 360 degrees in a pattern carry the distinctly charged energy of a planet. A rendezvous with one of our siblings, however, delivers an especially dynamic piece of time, and as anyone who studies time finds out, a tryst with Pluto is intense.

While some people speculate there is a more distant planet, at present Pluto has the outermost orbit. It plunges above and below the orbital plane formed by the other planets, and just now it is temporarily inside the orbit of Neptune.

With a diameter only about one-quarter the size of ours, this planet correlates with experiences of the most severe kind. It establishes that being far away and small do not diminish the intensity of a planet's effect.

Pluto is actually a double planet. Its moon is only 10,000 miles out, and almost as large as it is. Like two dancers grasping both hands as they lean outward and twirl around their common center, Pluto and Charon are locked in a face-to-face spin. Perhaps this motion has something to do with the tornadic qualities they produce in our lives.

With Pluto we step into a forceful magnetic field and respond to its draw as if we were a bed of iron filings splayed out on a plate. To some degree we are each a habit of random attachments, and Pluto's tractor beam issues a command to let go. Holding the proxy of death itself, Pluto is a powerful pull. Its process narrows the path and serves re-alignment with Being.

In a black hole compression, this space resonates with the Eighth House and concentrates our ability to stand alone. It elicits the tenacity necessary to withstand isolation, the ability to endure pain, and the relentless determination to stay alive during a difficult period.

Pluto confines the evolutionary force as a magnetic field confines particles. Encounters with this energy cleave us from passing circumstances to face our dependence on them. Though that serves our evolution, it can also shake our confidence. People often report anxiety and stress while processing this electromagnet in time. It resonates with *power*.

Unless we are saints, we are dependent on something, and indebtedness makes us vulnerable in a Plutonian space. Gordon discovered Pluto's unforgiving nature this way. Overextended and struggling to stabilize his financial empire, during a passage over this planet he missed a major loan payment for the first time. He was forced to re-structure his business, but because he dealt with his debt, he also came away from this brush with collapse leaner and stronger — and that is characteristic of Pluto.

While Pluto certainly challenges any false pride we might have by ripping away things we thought were ours, this local exposure to *power* does not remove any more than we can withstand or evolution would defeat itself. Rather, misalignments give way, and dependent bonds break.

When Janet felt Pluto's squeeze, she was helping a teacher organize a series of seminars. Though these two people had worked together for some time, their relationship fell into power struggles as she integrated this degree. He attacked her dependence on him, and she confronted her habit of giving her power away to men. She was facing her *lack* of power, and that can be very uncomfortable.

This strongest force concentrates, isolates and eliminates, and our entry into a context like this sometimes coincides with excruciating loss. Glenda was extremely close to her son and had gradually become emotionally dependent on him. But as she processed Pluto when he was eighteen years old, her son was killed in a car crash. It took years to adjust to this tragedy, of course, but eventually she was able to let her love for her son hold the tender new ground laid bare by their separation. This is a classic experience of Pluto.

Though facing dependence can be extremely painful, we can make sense of loss, at least, by understanding our process. Plutonian periods compress us to the core of who we are, sometimes removing what we erroneously feel we cannot do without. There we are forced to re-bind with our Being. You can hear the effects of a restructuring like this when people talk of being stronger for having survived difficult circumstances.

Bunny was thirty-nine years old as she approached her Pluto degree and says she was thinking about death at the time. As she passed over and drew away from this intersection between life and death, both her parents died.

Before you let fear set in, however, and wonder when this will happen to you, realize that we each interpret time according to our individual evolutionary needs. We take in Pluto's frequency in our own way. These appointments with *power* detach us, but that does not have to mean we have to call on death. This is a two-way street, as all conditions are, and if we can integrate it, an exchange with *power* can also be em*power*ing. Bunny recalls that time, too, for the inheritance she received.

If we could interview George Washington, he might report a similar episode. He lost his step-brother to illness during his Pluto passage, and at the same time inherited Mount Vernon.

Greed, possessiveness and jealousy might also attend this time, but they are not created in this process. They are our reactions to loss.

We can be transfer stations between life and death in as many ways as there are people. Camille's ex-boyfriend committed suicide when she passed over this degree. Ivy struggled to leave her abusive husband. Yet in this space-time, new life is also pushing through. Jane and Lester both became parents while stepping across this bridge.

Sometimes a Pluto encounter is about the subject of evolution itself. Though trained as an elementary school teacher, during her Pluto passage Emily took a job at a cancer research laboratory preparing molds for a study of their evolutionary process. Yet this energy is rarely that easy to integrate, and there was another aspect to her education in *power*. During this time she was also attacked and fought off a rapist. "I was stupid," she said. "I won't be that naive again." Being gullible is a lax and powerless state that is straightened up in a Pluto space.

Annie's Pluto is in her First House, so she integrates it when she addresses issues about her identity. "That's when I came out as a lesbian," she replied when I asked what was going on at the time. "I struggled with the decision to go public, but I remember it very clearly. That's when I owned up to who I really am."

Owning one's power is Plutonian, and when Pluto is a First House experience, its regeneration pushes up through our personal presentation.

If there is an archetype for this consciousness, it would be the samurai, the warrior able to face death and perform right action without attachment to the result.

It is best to face Plutonian situations head on. Midwesterners regularly encounter Plutonian conditions in the concentrated power of tornadoes. Yet they do not hide from knowing about them. They prepare and hunker down into their best awareness of what is necessary for the confrontation. In these events we draw inward, are tested, and carry on with a new regard for life.

As demanding as this integration may be, we are empowered by our survival of it. If you watch your life, you will see that Pluto's conditions also attend a birth.

JUPITER

Sometimes it is helpful to think of time as having a shape. It seems as if it does, and it can be understood that way. We could think of winter, for example, as applying a shape that contracts and draws life inward in cold weather.

The climate of personal time, too, seems to apply a shape. People processing Pluto or the Eighth House de-scribe periods of collapse, and they say things like "the ceiling in the den fell down," or "my confidence collapsed," or "I lost my business and I was crushed." I remember standing at the kitchen sink while trying to come up with a way to hold Pluto's variety of descriptions, and I had on a pair of oversized rubber gloves as I dipped my hands into the dishwater. The gloves pressed inward from all directions, and suddenly the pieces fell together. Experiences of Pluto cram toward the center as if the larger surrounding space were compressing. We behave as if it is.

People talk about Jupiter periods as expansions outward. Now they say things like, "I feel like I've been set free," or "I got away for a long vacation in Hawaii," or "I wanted to give something back to the community." Inside the Jupiter degree is a nugget of Ninth House consciousness, a bubble of *expansion*, and we billow out with it, swelling into 'the more' with its increase.

121

In this context, we either go out or give out, and the commodity moving through us here is information. We might increase its flow by travelling to some new or far-off place, or we might become a conduit for information by teaching what we ourselves have to give. In either case, Jupiter is a space in which we are informed: *by* new information if we are given to, and *with* new information if we ourselves do the giving.

The word *inform* describes this energy's capacity *to supply oneself with knowledge.* Both giving and receiving information will do that. Obviously we are informed when we receive information, but providing it also informs us in the sense that we are permeated by the very process of furnishing it, as anyone who teaches finds out. *Inform* has the added meaning *to animate or inspire* which alludes also to Jupiter's association with preachers and orators. This condition flows information.

The Jupiter space exists as a system. It presents the idea of data already in mutual communication, and we might say it is data in a social shape. Information systems are organic, they move, and they maintain a state of newness as ecosystems do. The Jupiter space seems held together in some common matrix — not information gathering, but information already assembled into a paradigm. Whereas growth through Pluto and the Eighth House is the result of compressive pressures, Jupiter is growth through the experience of a larger space.

This energy does not seem to make the indelible impression that some others do. Integrating it is often a pleasant experience, and perhaps when that is the case, there is no particular need to remember it. But like all energies, though you may have to take a wider view to see this one, when its time comes, it's there.

You might be informed by other cultures and philosophies. You might choose the social matrix of games and sports which themselves are organic systems. Or in another example of the two-way flow of energy, with the arrival of this one you might be the more-giver by disseminating information yourself through teaching, public speaking, broadcasting, or publishing.

The publishing world was Valerie's experience of Jupiter. Though she had been writing for only a few years, when she passed through this space she was given an advance to write a collection of poems and began negotiations with a publishing company to settle the terms of a contract to record her work. But that was not the full extent of her expression of this energy. Though she has had many jobs in her day, at that time she was supporting herself by writing profiles for a marketing company to announce the publication of books and videos. Marketing is a standard way of distributing information. It is a distinctly Jupiter idea.

The wider contact offered in this space comes in many varieties, of course, and here is one that illuminates the effects of an energy's House position. Linda's Jupiter is in her Fifth House where a fire is lit in the heart to initiate the creative process. Whether we go to it or it comes to us, Jupiter's new paradigms often come in the form of exposure to another culture, and when she processed her combination of expansion and heartspace, Linda fell in love with a foreigner. I wonder what his energy was doing.

Here is another type of information system. In her Jupiter space-time, Isabel felt a terrific need to get away from home and take a vacation, yet she could not afford to leave town. On what she thought was impulse, instead she bought a FAX-modem for her computer and filled that expanse by cruising the Internet, our newest information space.

The United States was pulling off its Jupiter in 1949 when an American made the first non-stop flight around the world. Long-distance travel has always been associated with Jupiter, and that is certainly the largest expansion into the faraway we could have made in those days.

Public officials add another dimension to understanding energies because they interact with the national psyche, as we saw reflected in General Eisenhower's decision to invade Europe when

America's birthprint offered up the space to begin. Now consider this remarkable chapter in our national political debate. Hillary Rodham Clinton was taking in her Jupiter when her husband was elected President. This planet was just below the horizon to her right when she was born, so in her pattern that combines information systems with the Sixth House condition of maintaining a state of health. Over the next year, while moving between Jupiter and her progressing Jupiter, she headed up a health care reform task force and planned her proposal for a new health care system.

Thomas Jefferson offers two beautiful examples of integrating Jupiter. During his first passage over this planet in 1790, he was appointed our first Secretary of State under President Washington. As envoys authorized to carry information for a nation, ministers of state embody the Jupiter principle. The word 'minister' means to give, and Jupiter has always been associated with statesmen. At his second passage over this planet in 1817, after planning and designing it himself, Mr. Jefferson was supervising the construction of the University of Virginia — while imbued with information dissemination again.

In the long run it is the process that matters. We take our lessons from both the yes and no responses to our efforts. A context of energy is about an idea, and the results of our experience with it depend on a mixture of factors, especially for political figures for whom the public's considerations are half of the equation. Though Mrs. Clinton's health plan did not become law, her experience of preparing it served our process as well as hers. As you may recall, the Sixth House is most often a statement of what *doesn't* work, and she held that space publicly for us.

THE RIGHT QUESTIONS

You will probably begin to hear what I call 'the right questions.' They are questions like, *What made him so interested in diet? Why did her career take off like that? Why do women only want to talk about relationships? Why would they get divorced after all these years? How did we arrive at this sea change in American politics?*

A lot of riddles are present simply because we are ignorant of our context. We do not know it's there, we don't know its characteristics, and we do not know the sequence of change.

All of humanity listens to this song. Whether it is art, history, economics, philosophy or personal evolution, whatever interests you have can be understood all over again inside the changing flow of conditions. Our participation in time is the grand drama of life.

Yet, as happens in true discovery, now a whole new set of questions arises. *What in the world is going on? How does this work? What generates these conditions? Why does the Moon unfold this process? What is the correlation between rotation and revolution? What happens when we leave the planet? Would we process Earth-time in space?*

We are taking our first look at the qualities that will educate a new civilization, and we will know them first in ourselves.

SATURN

So you get the idea now that planets are knobs of space-time, small local bundles of characteristics. They are all different, and astrologers collect clues about them by matching periods of contact with trails of evidence.

Saturn 'precipitates,' so it is likely you will be able to identify the effects of this planet. By precipitate I mean to make real, either in consciousness or in physical reality. Saturn retains and densifies, it preserves and conserves. It bestows form and definition.

In the body it shapes our skin, bones and teeth, and we experience this defining capacity in ourselves as the ability to make judgements.

Saturn has Tenth House characteristics. As an awareness, this energy is recognition and *acknowledgement*. We experience it as responsibility, and Saturn is the father archetype.

This planet produces a kind of orientation in consciousness, one that descends from high to low to form ideas like perspective and the ability to oversee. It orders things into vertical and linear hierarchies, so this planet relates to directorship in organizations. We call its precipitation through time *history*. We do not record everything that happens, just the events we choose to acknowledge, and those we list in a linear string.

Kenneth was passing through this part of his pattern and receiving his education in responsibility when he accidentally drove off the road and into deep water while giving a friend a lift home. Though he survived, his friend drowned, and that event colored his reputation in the community. As the accident became public, it was found that he left the scene without reporting what had happened. His delayed acknowledgement of the incident became an issue, and the extent to which he could take personal responsibility was brought forward in his Saturn degree.

Margot played her Saturn another way. At the time of its integration, her company was having trouble finding the right manager for their Hong Kong office, hiring several candidates who did not work out.

As she processed Saturn, however, Margot was promoted to a position that would put her in charge of this search. While she was acknowledged for the work she had done, she was also able to hire the manager who eventually succeeded in their Hong Kong operation. In her condition, she could recognize in someone else the Saturnian capacity her boss had also recognized in her.

The Saturn experience was more personal for Marie, however. Located just below the horizon to her left when she was born, Marie's Saturn is in a First House orientation. When she processed it she set out to deal with an aspect of her personality — a First House mode. Though her father had been dead for years, the discord she still felt between them was giving her problems in relationships. Marie made a 3,000 mile pilgrimage to her father's grave to settle things while she processed this planet. It was time to assume responsibility for the issues still resting with her father.

Also born with Saturn in a First House position, Catherine did nearly the same thing. As she approached this energy, she entered therapy to address problems she had with her father.

Do you recall that Veronica's mother died when she processed her Moon, the mother archetype? Rita's father died while she was processing Saturn, the father archetype. How do a parent and child synchronize two lives like that? Some grand design must be setting these dramas into motion. Energy patterns actually increase our faith in a Master Plan.

While mothers hold who-we-are-to-ourselves-alone, our sense of self, fathers hold the ability to recognize and be responsible. So when we assume the space that both parents held for us as children, we internalize these two conditions as self responsibility. By knowing time's qualities, we can deepen this process and begin to separate from the conditioning we carry.

Sometimes we can feel an energy coming, even discern how far away it is, and Rachel could feel her approach to Saturn. She is an artist, and when she neared this degree she was developing story-boards for an animated film she was planning. I knew she was about six months ahead of this encounter so I asked her what the film was about. "It's still in the planning stage," she said, "but it's about a con-man named Justice who goes around dispensing lessons of right and wrong." I told her about Saturn's correspondence with judgement, and we both howled with laughter.

When it is time to integrate a frequency, whether to accept or refuse it is up to us, and we make of it what we will. But we do not get to choose whether it is present or not. That has already been determined. Any one of these people could find a whole spectrum of issues coalescing around Saturn when its time comes.

I have already told you about studying history while I was processing this planet, but there were other events descending through this space while I was taking it in. Saturn also rang a heavy sense of judgement in me.

In my imprint, this planet has Third House correlations with communication and the hands, and that had some striking manifestations. I was having a difficult time communicating with one of my co-workers. I could not seem to drop my judgements about the way she did her job.

One morning I woke up with skin blotches the size of 50-cent pieces all over my abdomen, and I knew the communication that was not happening between us was popping out through that rash. It persisted for six weeks — until I pulled off my Saturn degree. Then it was gone.

Next someone with mental problems wandered into our office and began quizzing me about people on our staff. When I hesitated, he hissed at me, "Who ever told you you could communicate!" Communication and judgement again, even from someone walking in off the street.

Then a cyst appeared at the base of one of my fingers, and there is my Saturn's association with the hands. Now my judgements were localizing there, and they felt like a stone inside. Though I do not have a formal religious affiliation, I do have a Christian background, and while I was doing the dishes on Easter morning I was listening to a radio program about Jesus and the resurrection. Still thinking about the judgements I was dealing with at work, I asked to have this weight lifted from my heart. As I leaned down to pick up my cat's dish from the floor, in that very instant the cyst broke. My judgements and that cyst were held by the same condition — and in that moment they both disappeared.

I happened to visit my mother during my passage over this planet, too, and quite by accident, if there is such a thing, I became interested in my family history. I noticed a book on the bedside table called *Past Made Present* written by my great-grandfather while he was a Presbyterian minister. He had written that book to record the history of the church in its first fifty years, and you would think that would be dull as dirt. I read the whole book in one sitting. Right there in bed in my mother's house, I felt like the period on the family sentence. In that small pocket of my life, after being totally disinterested in my lineage, I comprehended who my mother's family were and my place in the flow of generations. I could feel Saturn's linear shape like an arrow pointing right to me.

I realized I was processing Saturn as it was happening, so I noticed things I probably would not have, like that cyst. These short infusions of planetary energy do not last very long, but they are little gold mines of potential realization and growth. If we are aware of them as they play through us, we can use them to become more conscious. We already are.

URANUS

Ah, Uranian energy. This frequency is popping out every-where as our planet enters its new 2,000-year-long condition. Each individual, every generation and all forms of life are sailing into Uranian space as the new civilization sweeps in worldwide.

The discombobulating change we are coping with now is our collective experience of crossing the bowshock into living time. Energy here discharges like a beacon flashing now-now-now, and the new frequency startles us awake with speed bumps that disconnect us from the past.

Though they both relate to time, the Uranian kind of change is completely different from the Saturnian form of time strung out behind us as history. We receive Uranus in sudden jolts, like getting an elbow in the ribs when nodding off in public.

Uranian people are the mad scientists of the world, the eccentric, wild-haired geniuses who strike out on their own. They look a little kooky, and they hang out with z-words like zany, zippy, zooie, zappy, and electrizzzzity. Uranian types are free and individually plugged in to an intuitive mental creativity.

I am delighted when the effects of a planet are like its physical characteristics. If you had to identify this planet in a lineup at the police station, you could — it looks a little kooky, too. All the other planets would be standing upright, and Uranus would be gyrating on the floor, its magnetic field flailing like the arms and legs of someone rolling around in flames trying to put out the fire. This renegade nonconformist wheels around the Sun on its side, its ring system making it a bull's-eye in space.

Uranian jolts prod pent-up resistance to suddenly break free. Earth expresses this in earthquakes and lightning, and at the intensity that we humans can handle, we receive these Uranian discharges as insights. Its pathway is intuition, and Uranus fuels the human mind with *truth*, the Eleventh House experience of what is.

As a continuous current, Uranian disconnection serves the development of freedom and autonomy. America's Moon — who we are to ourselves alone — resonates with this quality. That makes us think of ourselves as a free people.

Knowing that a friend of mine was integrating this frequency, I called her while it was most intense to see if she might have had some collision with surprise. She said she had had a jarring day, that a fellow teacher had burst into her classroom to deliver a message. It turns out the message was not important, her experience was entirely about being so abruptly interrupted. Behind that intrusion was a Uranian goose into the now.

This kind of interruption boosts us out of hypnotic addictions. Habits are little historical chains of behavior, and they are broken, too, by this frequency. Lou stopped drinking while processing this energy. Russell joined Alanon to deal with his wife's alcohol addiction. We become more independent when we integrate the discontinuities Uranus delivers.

By promoting an independent point of view, Uranian energy also supplies the freedom inventors and artists need to create. Though she had never worked as a commercial artist before, as Lorraine processed this planet she was selected by her company to be Head of their Creative Department. "I don't know why they chose me," she said, "it just came out of the blue." That phrase describes many Uranian experiences, and for what it's worth, Uranus is blue.

As I approached this planet, I had a revelation that transformed my understanding of time. I had come into contact with a group of people who already thought of themselves as a spectrum of inner Light, and we had a common language. I did a string of sessions with a number of them within a few short months, and it was through their feedback that I realized we are processing our own birthprints. I had been looking at static moments before, trying to 'read' what they meant. But with my arrival at Uranus, the birthprint morphed into one continuous process of change. I could see we were integrating our patterns.

I felt as if I had stubbed my toe on a cosmic doorsill and stumbled inside of time. Those sessions brought me into synchrony with change itself, and that happened while I was integrating my Uranian degree.

Even as a nation we experienced this bolt of electricity as time to synchronize our watches. Standard time was proposed shortly after the country integrated this planet at the end of 1783. And standard time became law 134 years later when Uranus in the sky moved across the Moon's position in America's birthprint. The Uranian condition brings us all into the same timeframe: living, changing *now*.

Uranus is a pacemaker: break-break-break into the present. Not precipitate-precipitate into the past as Saturn does, but disengage from history altogether. As this condition gooses our new civilization into real time, we press our computers to speed up, and we grow impatient with the few seconds our old models take to process information. We want quicker access, faster downloading, speedier connections to everything, and more space to store the old information we are dumping behind.

When we ourselves encounter this quality, we begin losing our memories and dropping our personal histories as well in order to lighten up and keep up with the now. It is making us all more autonomous — not only more independent from others in the present, but more independent from our own history, too.

Uranian time prompts idioms like *give me a break, I'm out of here, out of the blue, tell it like it is, do your own thing, lighten up*, and ideas like *the end of history*. From here we see the past for what it is, and we do not live there any more.

We live in real time now, planetary time, and change will stop being a jarring experience as we synchronize with it.

NEPTUNE

If Uranus has the effect of waking us up, what we are waking up from is Neptunian. Neptune resonates with deep unconsciousness, and this planet tunes to the world of sleep and spirit.

Neptune relates to vistas at their largest, and the Neptune degree is a small pocket of the big Twelfth House space of *oneness*. It's the whispered "Ooooooo!" of turning our eyes upward to the stars on a dark night.

This frequency correlates with the unmanifest part of the spectrum through which we absorb ideals, dreams and meaning. It *de*-focuses the attention as if dilating the pupils to broaden our access to a larger whole.

Transcending physical reality, Neptune inspires understanding and forgiveness. It heightens our belief in possibilities, and seekers, imagineers and idealists keep company with this ethereal energy. It resonates with the Pisces civilization now disappearing behind us.

When Morgan processed this local vein of inspiration one summer, she had what some call a peak experience. "I was thirteen, and I was on the farm under a beautiful tree at the bottom of the paddock. I felt surrounded by the spirit of my grandfather, and his presence and a light came around me. In that afternoon I understood the universe, god and everything." Morgan was permeated with spiritual understanding while passing through the measureless space of her Neptune degree.

Because Neptune offers direct contact with understanding, these experiences are usually so profound that we want to communicate them somehow. That day had such an impact on Morgan that she remembers writing a poem about it, and poetry is the form we most often use to translate our impressions of this elusive place. Through poems we capture our immersions into the beyond with metaphors of the more familiar.

Poets have always been found communing with Neptune. We experience meaning in its reservoir of *oneness*, and poets attempt to mediate that with symbols and images. Isn't that what English teachers have always asked, "What did the poet *mean* by that?" Poets are familiar with the meaning in Neptune's invisible world, but if you remember English class, most people are not. The rest of us receive our poetry lessons from time.

In this largest space, we sense that all points of view belong, and this frequency induces us to consider what has been left out. Approaching our Neptune at the end of 1791, from this lofty state of mind our countrymen re-evaluated their dream and added the Bill of Rights to our Constitution that year.

During these periods we think in terms of the ideal, and when the United States integrated Neptune again in 1955, we made that a real place — Disneyland opened its gates.

We crossed Neptune again in 1983 when President Reagan proposed Star Wars, his strategic defense initiative. In a little more than every twenty-seven years, we add some portion of idealism — or perhaps fantasy — to our country's development when we process this frequency.

The physical underpinnings of life might erode as we turn our attention to the largest whole, however, and finding ourselves awash in this energy can bring on a period of drowning confusion.

Peggy spent the months of her Neptune encounter in painful re-evaluation of her relationships with men. Having just been dropped by the man in her life, she hired a therapist to help her recover from depression and make a new sense of things. It was time to gain, and receive, understanding.

Though this often marks a time of dissolution, the meaning we access here is part of our education as Beings. Even nature drops hints that a bigger reality exists than the one that we can see. The human race long ago discovered that psychedelic plants transport us to this dreamscape, and we brew alcohol in an attempt to do that ourselves.

Though Neptune resonates with the Twelfth House part of the sky just above the horizon at the left, if you were born when it was overhead, you would slip into its magnification while processing the most public piece of space-time. Princess Diana has Neptune there, and she married precisely while passing through this heavenly glow of idealism. Out of a twenty-seven-year cycle, she was just twenty-one days past the peak of this rapture, essentially right in it on her wedding day. Millions watched the Prince marry the Princess in the space from which dreams are made and fairy tales are told. Because Neptune is in her Tenth House, Princess Diana's public persona is spritzed with enchantment, and we will probably always see her through a mist of idealism.

Another playing this publicly romantic part, Grace Kelly was also born when Neptune was overhead. It's the perfect picture of a princess.

Franklin Roosevelt was bathing in idealism, too, when he married, integrating the very degree of his Neptune when he wed Eleanor in 1905. The Democratic Party also saw him in that light when they nominated him for President in the summer of 1932 as he passed through that same degree again.

But Neptune is the antithesis of bodily vitality, and its de-focusing can leave one physically depleted. Dissolution changes the tuning from the body to the spirit and leaves us physically vulnerable, as we are when we are asleep. So sometimes sickness is induced in a Neptune time. Its symptoms relate to the devitalization itself, and problems here are not easy to diagnose.

Those who carry an emphasis of this frequency in their basic patterns have probably never been physically strong. I got scarlet fever while taking it in as a child, and my sister came down with multiple sclerosis when she processed this energy.

But of course illness is not the only possibility. Neptune merely diffuses us into the universal space we all hold in common as Beings, and that reduces our individually focused vitality.

After 2,000 years the general population has been saturated with this frequency as the Pisces wave crests and floods the twentieth century. The communal space of television, the lure of escape through drugs, a bloated population, a debilitated armed response from the immune system rendering us vulnerable to vague sicknesses like chronic fatigue and AIDS, as well as a desire for spiritual enlightenment are all at high water marks. Now, one by one, we are waking up from our spiritual baptism to take up residence in real time.

A Larger Perception

Now that we have seen spaceship Earth, we seem to be ready for a larger picture of ourselves, too.

The global consciousness that accompanies locating ourselves in time switches us from a linear reality to a spherical one, from the dead time of history to the living time of now, and from doing to Being. Correlating the day with the year changes our center of reference from the Earth to the Sun where we emulate the Sun's creative force through our own creative self actualization.

Time is the school for our continuing education, and it is the most democratic schoolroom there is. Everyone attends class, and though no two students take the exact same concentration of courses, we are all exposed to the same ideas.

Some future generation will ask why this works. Our generation is given a fantastic process that relates us to our planet and the planetary family, and out of that is coming a global awareness. For now, that is enough.

Encountering Progressed Planets

So there you have the effects of planetary energies. Each has its own process, and you will integrate the whole lot every twenty-seven years. Each delivers a condition with specific characteristics, and it is we who translate them into thought and action.

With the arrival of a given piece of time, we transpose its qualities through a corresponding range of effects while tuning to some portion of its array. Lists of terms describing the correlations we generally make are in Appendices at the back.

I should remind you that all the planets progress, not just the Moon, though even over a whole lifetime the other planets do not progress very far. So upon processing a planet's original degree, we encounter its progressed position shortly thereafter, anywhere from a few weeks later for the outer planets, to a few years later in the case of the faster-moving inner ones.

Neptune, for instance, moves very little in ninety days, and it progresses through only that much of our pattern in ninety years of life. Mercury, however, moves much faster, so by the age of ninety it could take close to eleven years to traverse the space between its original and progressed positions.

A planet and its progressed position carry the same characteristics, however, so processing an outer planet like Neptune can bring on a Neptunian period five or six months long. After feeling our approach to it from several months out, we pass through its space, then encounter its progressed position some weeks later and slowly pull away. The distance between these two positions all depends on a planet's motion in the sky after our birth, and the speeds of the planets vary.

At the rate of taking in a day's worth of change over a year, we integrate forty days of sky-change in forty years of life, fifty days in fifty years, eighty days of motion in eighty years of life. Whatever is in the degree we are integrating colors our experience, including planets transiting through the sky right now.

Computers can chart all this for us, and the programs are already written.

POLARITY AND OPPOSITIONS

While the correlations between life and our solar system have been collected over thousands of years, there have been so many changes over the last hundred years that we now find we have to re-define our interpretations of the sky, too.

We have immensely increased our personal awareness through various therapies, through meditation and increased communication, and we need to re-state our experience of time in concepts large enough for us now. We have outgrown the notion of birthprints as static patterns to which things happen, and we cannot relate to ideas smaller than we are.

In translating the effects of time to larger concepts, however, something amazing happens. Positions opposite each other in space-time form a polarity as well in consciousness. Polar ideas have a direct relationship — as the one increases, so does the other — and they require each other.

Take the concept of *will*. We cannot know how we project ourselves without being mirrored back, and *will* can only be experienced through *reflection*, its opposite concept in the circle imprinted from the sky.

Trust, commitment, is the polar opposite of *power*. A fire hose has no power if it is flailing around spewing water every which way. It is useless until someone takes hold of it and *commits* to spraying something specific, until it is entrusted to something. In the same way, personal power is a function of keeping one's commitments. While doing so develops the kind of trust we experience inside as stability, other people also learn they can rely on us to do as we say we will. From either idea, the one relates to the other.

Communication relates directly to its polar complement, *expansion*. Associating information forms the social network into which we extend ourselves. And conversely, by extending ourselves, we increase our exposure to new information and our communication with it.

Acknowledgement allows us to perceive and include aspects of *Self*, its polar companion. Recognition allows us to know who we are. Or stated from the opposite position, the integration of qualities into Self requires that we acknowledge what those qualities are.

In order to *create* — to actualize ourselves — we need to tell the *truth*. We can only actualize what is already so, what is true. And telling the truth opens the heart, the space from which we create.

Oneness requires *choice*. If it is not to overwhelm our linear reality, oneness must be processed. It is the ocean from which we make selections, including the selection of nutrients from food. Health means 'whole,' one, and an idea like holistic health states the relationship between these two. They manifest each other. Choosing our way through daily life is our physical expression of *oneness*.

That two ideas opposite each other in space-time work in tandem seems — well, magical. But if duality is the way this planet works, complements make sense. Up requires down, positive implies negative, and male needs female. Even DNA, the material that builds our biology, is formed from pairs of bases at the molecular level.

For our purposes, duality validates that these concepts are in fact correct. They operate in couplets and require each other in a planetary medium that we already know manifests in pairs.

Yet it is not just concepts that operate in pairs. Specific degrees do, too. As we process each degree, we elicit the exact opposite one at the same time. If there is a planetary sibling there, we process it, too, and again something fascinating happens. Whereas we resonate with an energy *in*ternally when we move over it, opposite degrees appear to come through circumstances outside of us.

I mentioned earlier that I earned my teaching certificate and set out to teach school while moving over my own Jupiter, which carries the idea of expansion that we often transpose to education. When I moved opposite Jupiter fourteen years later, however, I met the person I consider my teacher. Out of 360 possible degrees, I was in the one exactly opposite this planet when I met her, and our first appointment was two days after that opposition.

This is a fascinating story. I should tell you the rest of it just for fun. A friend and I had decided to attend a lecture about the soul and its evolution, but on the day it was to be given I got the flu and had to stay in bed. My friend went without me, and afterwards I asked about the talk and what the speaker was like. She said I would probably like to meet this person, and she told me her name. Though I had never heard of her, I realized I had just bought a book about this woman, solely on impulse because it had fallen off the shelf at my feet as I was browsing in a bookstore. I made an appointment to see her, and when she opened the door I knew her instantly. Our association began that day. But had I gone to the lecture as I originally planned, I would not have been in the degree opposite my Jupiter. I guess it was not time to meet yet.

Here is another story about oppositions I especially like. If you will recall, Saturn resonates with history, responsibility and the father archetype. I was teaching myself history when I integrated this energy a few years ago, and my education was coming up through me, internally, as I began to collect an outline of what happened when.

At that time I knew I was processing Saturn, but I did not know I was integrating it when I opposed it fourteen years earlier. Then I was taking a personal development seminar, and completing relationships from the past was part of the work required. This time I dealt with Saturnian conditions *external* to me. My family was divorced so I did not grow up with my father, and I had given up a certain amount of my responsibility for our relationship. During my opposition to Saturn, however, I talked with him and took that responsibility back. Fathers and responsibility are both typical translations of this kind of consciousness, and though I was completely unaware of integrating it, our repair had come due in time.

Because patterns can emphasize vastly different issues, the events one person is dealing with can be shocking to someone else. Elaine, for instance, is set up to get an education in *power*, and she had a difficult experience of it when she moved opposite this idea.

In her pattern, Venus — reflection through another person — is included in her Eighth House experience of *power*, and when she moved opposite that Venus the man she was seeing was murdered. His hands were chopped off and his face was obliterated. While this event is horrifying, violence is part of power's spectrum, and Elaine was operating in that arena. Whatever our reaction to this may be, her brush with death came through external circumstances while she was integrating power and relationship in the polar opposite degree.

Events like this probably arise from our personal histories. Through our experience of time's conditions, we elicit what we already associate with specific energies and come to terms with what we experience through them. Reaping one's karma may be as simple, and real, as taking a walk through time.

145

It is our job to steer a course through life, and we are always at choice. But the choices we make establish a private climate inside us. We experience ourselves as being somewhere in the range from good to bad by the choices we have already made, and we have to live inside our skins. Maybe this is the basis for ideas like 'vengeance is mine, sayeth the Lord.' Most people who have done horrible things suffer long past the events themselves. We might even choose to experience injury just to come to some kind of balance or resolution inside. 'Do unto others as you would have them do unto you' certainly serves our own peace of mind as much as anyone else's.

If we knew the path was already there, we could drop the habit of complaining. There is nothing you, nor anyone else, can do to change the pattern into which you were born and your ongoing integration of it. That choice has already been made.

THE NODAL AXIS

Now you have a generic understanding of the conditions that shape a life. We have holographed the sky in twelve partitions; the planets have been projected onto us as if lit from behind; and starting from birth, our configuration progresses slowly forward, while the Progressing Moon knits it all together into one developing experience of Self.

And here is the linchpin: the entire pattern matures through two opposite points. While we get an education through every energy, one polarity dominates, and our lives seem to have a basic theme that we play out through a pair of ideas.

It might be learning to commit one's power, or shed control for trust; maybe it is choosing ultimate values, or balancing separation with relationship; perhaps it is to assume more responsibility. Our growth organizes around a pair of ideas opposite each other in spacetime.

Since there are twelve ideas in all, and each one has an abundance of possibilities, there is a wide variety of interpretations we could make of these concepts. But our experience at these two poles will illustrate how we are steering our way between them, and moving over one of them will bring up issues that make a new sense fourteen years later when we integrate the other. These two points are the Moon's nodes, where the Moon's orbit intersects our own.

The whole process of integrating a birthprint is based on the Moon, so it is not surprising that its nodes hold an idea central to our evolution.

To understand what they are, however, in your mind retreat to a high vantage point where you can see the Earth and Moon together from space. There is the Moon, circling us once every month while we are zooming along around the Sun. The Moon's path is inclined to ours by about five degrees, and that means every month it crosses our course twice — once going north and once going south. We don't know why these points would produce effects, too, but they certainly are a powerful completion to this process.

Though any two polar points in a pattern operate in tandem, something special goes on in this axis. What we are developing here has a direction to it — the idea at the South Node is maturing at the North Node. Here is one woman's experience of them.

Loretta's South Node imprinted in the part of her pattern holding *acknowledgement*. South Nodes are somehow 'complete,' and being recognized as the right person for responsible positions has always come easily to her. Loretta is a natural at taking care of things and she realizes that, but as she expressed it herself, *she feels she doesn't know who she is*. At the opposite node she is developing *self perception*. These two are a polar pair.

As Loretta integrated her South Node and the acknowledgement and responsibility stored there, she became totally exhausted and physically depleted. "I was working too hard and was just worn out," she said. Because the development in this axis is directional, eventually South Nodes produce only the need to realize the polar concept, and Loretta seems to have had no more room to assume responsibility for others. She is experiencing the South Node's glass-full syndrome here. "I just went home and slept," she said. "It was the right thing to do."

Through her North Node, Loretta is learning to apply that sense of responsibility to herself, too. "I was taking care of everyone but me," she said. She is moving naturally into a greater self perception.

Loretta has had only three experiences of her nodes so far, and though the idea of taking care of herself is clearly there, her development of self responsibility is still in its early stages.

Mary, however, is eighty-one years old and has crossed this axis six times, so we can look at more examples of how the idea in her nodes is developing.

Mary's ripe South Node carries the concept of *will* — projection through the body, separation into an identity, and the experience of initiative. She was fourteen the first time she crossed this point, and that year she became seriously ill with rheumatic fever. Left physically weak, her early life revolved around being sick. That first South Node episode was an experience of her body.

She describes her second passage over the South Node twenty-seven years later as a major turning point. "I was getting a divorce from someone very rigid, and I like to try new things, so we had almost nothing in common. That's when I started a new life." This time she expressed that South Node projection by pulling away from a marriage that was not working, expressing her *will* through separation.

While searching her memory for the third crossing which occurred in her late sixties, she exclaimed, "Oh, that's when I really stuck my neck out, I started a bank." This time integrating her South Node produced a daring new venture, and she struck out on her own again.

All three of Mary's South Node experiences are demonstrations of *will*. First it was the *vehicle consciousness* brought on by her bout with rheumatic fever; next it was the *separation* of leaving her husband and her life as the wife of a university dean; and finally it was the *initiative* it takes to open a bank at the age of sixty-eight. Our ability to separate from communal spirit, to project ourselves into a vehicle, and to direct our attention is the sum total of *will*. Every time Mary processed her South Node she played an aspect of this idea.

To see how she has moved into the polar quality, *reflection*, let's look at occurrences at her opposite North Node. This node contains an idea we are growing into, and Mary integrated it the first time while in her late twenties.

"My twins were born then, and they gave me a reason for living, something to do with myself," she said. She saw her children as beneficiaries of the assertive ability she already had, as something to do with that highly developed will.

While moving over her North Node the next time, her children by then were twenty-seven years old, and she was taking care of her second husband who was in declining health. "He was a very nice person, he settled me down and gave a shape to my life. Before that I was just bouncing around." Apparently this man accommodated her strong sense of initiative, and she went on to describe this crossing as a period she again associates with doing for someone else.

In the circle of energy, *will* is complemented by *reflection*, and over her lifetime Mary is increasing her awareness through relationship. While experiences that require *will* occurred at her South Node, things to do, or people to do for, appeared at her North Node. Through her nodal axis she is applying herself to others.

She is about to integrate that North Node again, so I asked her what is on the horizon. She said she is tired of running a bank and is looking for something more worthwhile to do. "I want to write a book that will help children become aware of health," she said. "I know what it's like to be a sick child." Again, doing for other people is coming up, and this time she is including her first South Node experience with rheumatic fever as a child. You can see a sort of balancing out happening here. Mary seems to be conscious of both poles now as she processes that North Node again.

The ideas in the nodes are determined at birth by where they imprint in our pattern. The Moon's orbit is wobbling like a quarter tossed onto a table, making a loop once every nineteen years, so the points where it touches the table (or crosses the Earth's path) change. In addition, the Earth rotates through day and night below these two points, and they pass daily over all 360 degrees of our globe until captured in a birthprint.

Projected down onto the Earth when Roberta was born, these points imprinted just below the horizon at her right, and just above the horizon to her left — in her Sixth and Twelfth Houses. Roberta is coming out of the idea of mastering *choice*, and dissolving into the Twelfth House condition of universal spirit, *oneness* and unconditional love.

Although the ideas in a nodal axis develop over a whole lifetime, as soon as we experience two poles we can begin to accumulate some understanding of its translation in our lives. Roberta is set up so that her Progressing Moon crossed her North Node first, so let's look at what happened there.

She processed this node's de-focusing condition when she was only ten years old and in the fourth grade. "That was the year I lost my vision," she said. "I didn't want to see the violence in my home. I spent the whole year at school just listening because I couldn't see." Roberta's alcoholic father was regularly beating her mother, and these circumstances framed her experience of unconditional love. That kind of chaos in the physical environment often serves to force a Twelfth House retreat inward.

Roberta integrated this idea a second time when she was thirty-six. "I was working in advertising," she said, "and I had trouble with my eyes again that year." Upon having her eyes checked, the doctor told her she was losing her peripheral vision. The Twelfth House de-focusing condition produced vision problems again.

But look at this exquisite immersion into the world of unconditional love accompanying her loss of sight this time.

During her passage over this Twelfth House node, she entered into silence for a three-month retreat at a meditation center. "There was no eye contact there at all, so I could take my contact lenses out for the whole time, and I could rest my eyes."

She *was* resting her eyes, but she was also forgoing the individual separation we project through them. Instead, she entered the spiritual realm where we unite with unconditional love.

Eventually the retina of one eye collapsed. That is a pretty debilitating development, but unconditional love and acceptance is also a pretty lofty goal. So let's see what Roberta is bringing into this awareness from the mature South Node.

Located in the area of her pattern about *choice*, Roberta's Sixth House South Node correlates with what she does for a living. Her earliest experience there was of getting her first good job. "I got into sales for the first time then, and that was a great job." Her competence in the work world was already up and running well, which is typical of how south nodes operate.

Yet when I talked to her as she approached that node again, she said she had recently been laid off and was concerned about finding another position. Though she did find another, "a plum," she says of a sales position with the Los Angeles Philharmonic, within months she became disillusioned, feeling this job, too, was not working out.

South Node experiences eventually do nothing but propel us into North Node consciousness. Roberta was beginning a new relationship with someone who found it difficult to support her while she was not working, yet she felt it was most important to be accepted unconditionally during this time, whether she had an income or not. The glass-full syndrome is beginning to appear at her South Node. Being laid off energized Roberta's issue of acceptance.

It would be nice to have a formula for what she should do about this, and the universal one is to recognize the context for what is happening. *Oneness* and unconditional love are developing inside of Roberta, and this is part of her discovery that acceptance is an issue for her. Fourteen years from now she will integrate that North Node again, with a greater perspective on its roots in her childhood and an even larger sense of Self.

My South Node is coming in through the idea of *self percep-tion*. I first noticed that the Moon *is* perception, and that the Progressing Moon is our evolving perception, when I integrated that part of my birthprint and started this research. Perception matures through *acknowledgement* and validation at my North Node, and the Progressing Moon has brought me an immense amount of confirmation. It validated my own experience first.

For the United States, the idea complete at our South Node is independence and autonomy, and we take freedom as a given. We were processing this idea in 1994 when we voted to reduce the role of government and began de-centralizing federal power to deliver more autonomy to the states.

We are maturing through the polar concept of *creative self actualization*, so America is a country built to develop a self actualized people. The United States provides the freedom to become ourselves, and new immigrants know this best. In our growth as a nation we will eventually balance the liberty we hold dear with the self expression of inventors, artists and entrepreneurs. That sounds like us, doesn't it.

Issues have already been given to us through the internal conditioning of time. As events are generated around the nodal axis, we can see how we address these dominant concerns. We cannot go around them and we cannot hold them back, and we can process the nodal ideas in a positive or negative way. But imagine the world we could have if we fulfilled ourselves and our national potentials as well.

The Signs

There is another level of time we have not looked at yet so as to keep this simple. The measure around our planet — the space we divide into Houses — is in some very elegant correspondence with our revolution around the Sun.

There is room here for some brave physicist to address our correlation with time and discover why the characteristics measured around our planet also appear in twelve segments again during our planet's trip around the Sun. Rotation and revolution equate. There is something generic about 'going-around.'

The changes that occur as we revolve around the Sun, however, are too slow for us to take as our basic measure of time. Human beings seem to be tuned to a certain speed, and we relate to days.

Yet Earth does not have days, it has both day and night all the time, and Earth's version of a time-of-day is a season-of-the-year. When the ancients talked about the appearance of a set of stars in the sky and assigned names to them, they were referring to times of year, and what we call *Signs* are characteristics associated with seasons.

This larger level of change imprints on us, too, but just as climate is less immediate than the fluctuations of daily weather, Signs are secondary to Houses. They deliver a layer of underlying characteristics.

The Signs can imprint anywhere in our pattern, and a computer can generate a timeline for our passage through them, too. To recognize their characteristics, we only need to know the House to which each pertains, and here are the correlations. The Houses have the same characteristics as these Signs.

The First House	Aries
The Second House	Taurus
The Third House	Gemini
The Fourth House	Cancer
The Fifth House	Leo
The Sixth House	Virgo
The Seventh House	Libra
The Eighth House	Scorpio
The Ninth House	Sagittarius
The Tenth House	Capricorn
The Eleventh House	Aquarius
The Twelfth House	Pisces

It is difficult to picture a time of year as part of our birthprint without being off the planet, but if you were born looking out at the early winter portion of our orbit, those qualities would be added to the overhead portion of your pattern. Sagittarius or Ninth House characteristics would have imprinted there, too, but from further out, so to speak, and they would be part of your experience of *acknowledgement*.

Randy has this configuration, and when she processed her Tenth House, *acknowledgement*, she was at long last recognized by her department as the person who should run a new program at the university. But what program? The Sagittarius which had also imprinted there relates to information dissemination. She was tapped to head up an international network for instructing teachers on how to use telecommunications. Bingo.

In another Tenth House combination, here is Dana's experience of blending *acknowledgement* with a Sign. Emerging from a divorce and looking for work, she applied for a position at a small midwestern college. Though she did not have the advanced degree usually required, the Chairman of the Music Department recognized her abilities and hired her to teach piano solely on the basis of her superb technique. The Virgo time of year had also imprinted there, which added *choice* to that part of her birthprint — a major result of which is technique.

Of all the examples of sign energies, however, these two are jewels. Two sparkling expressions of Aquarius have become part of our national psyche. The Aquarian frequency adds truth, freedom, human rights, equality, independence and democracy to a pattern, and two of our countrymen have contributed their interpretations of it. With explicit clarity, Thomas Jefferson was processing Aquarius when he wrote the Declaration of Independence.

> *"We hold these truths to be self-evident, that all men are created equal, that they are endowed by their Creator with certain unalienable Rights, that among these are Life, Liberty and the pursuit of Happiness."*

And Abraham Lincoln was integrating this frequency when he chose its association with democracy to champion those who died in battle at Gettysburg:

> *"... government of the people, by the people, for the people, shall not perish from the Earth."*

The words of these two men have had an enormous impact on how we perceive ourselves as a country, and each was stating ideas in synchrony with his own process. Here is more evidence of the significance that attaches to being in resonance with time.

We have in fact walked part of every President's path with him, and while these two national leaders made significant contributions of their evolutionary lessons, not everyone rises to the occasion. We strolled with Richard Nixon, too, through his confrontive Eighth House lessons in *power*.

And finally, here is a beautiful example of the way a resonance that is held by a House is also characteristic of one of the Signs.

The Twelfth House and Pisces both release us into the timeless beyond of universal *oneness*. At the moment our ambassadors landed on the Moon for humanity's supreme experience of the oneness of Earth, in July of 1969 the United States was processing Pisces; Buzz Aldrin was integrating Pisces; and Neil Armstrong was passing through his Twelfth House.

In resonance with transcendent peace, we even left our first extraterrestrial footprint at a site called Tranquility Base.

That is all simply stunning.

When I was new to this, it seemed to me astrologers were drawing correlations between time and events that were pretty thin. I thought they were stretching things, and I wondered how they could assign any relevance at all to such obscure relationships.

Now I do that myself. The firm subtleties of time eventually overwhelm all of us who begin our studies of this fascinating subject in doubt, if not in total disdain.

PROCESSING SCORPIO

Of the twelve Signs, we are going to single out a few examples of Scorpio because it is so difficult to handle. It seems to be hard for everyone to integrate.

Scorpio resonates with the Eighth House: *power*, control and evolution. It often brings experiences with death. Its frequency strips one down to essence where only the core of who we are seems to escape the chaos of leaving behind what we must.

I have only seen one person take in this frequency without major disruption, and even she lost her grandmother while tuning to this idea. Going through it is like being re-born without actually dying.

We process all Sign energies as part of a House, of course, and if you imprinted Scorpio in the Eleventh House, it would be part of your experience of friendship. Belinda's pattern is set up this way. When she entered Scorpio there, two of her friends died, neither of them elderly.

President Franklin Roosevelt had Scorpio underlying his Second House, and during his experience there of *trust* and commitment, Eleanor discovered his affair with Lucy Mercer.

Recently married, Beth was just three months into Scorpio when her husband died in a plane crash.

James went through a divorce, lost his job, and his best friend died as well. "This has been the worst year of my life," he moaned.

Scorpio was part of Jill's First House association with the personality, and the very month she began processing it, she uprooted her whole life to move across the country and begin a most intense form of psychotherapy.

While life seems to get darker during a Scorpio time, like therapy, this is a darkness that serves us in the long run. Scorpio has the effect of changing us in a major way, as the Eighth House does, and as difficult as this might be, it brings on a period of accelerated evolution. Here we are forced to drop what is out of integrity, out of sync, or does not belong with us any more.

If you are having a bad patch in life, you could be undergoing your own transformation.

GALILEO

I subscribe to a data service. Every month I receive birth dates and times for public figures and people currently in the news. Recently included was a copy of a sheet of paper on file at the Library of Florence on which Galileo had drawn his birth pattern from his own calculations.

Though Galileo of course was Italian, the notes are written in math and astrological symbols, and that page is perfectly readable. Poring over it is like having a conversation across 400 years of time, and I felt as if I were sitting next to him as he uncovered the pattern we both knew would govern his experience of life.

Looking at a chart for the first time is always an exciting moment, but looking over the shoulder of this person as he scratched those markings is a wonderfully intimate experience. He knew both versions of the science of heaven, and in those calculations he shares not just an understanding of the motions of the sky, but revelations of a most personal kind.

Galileo was seventy years old when he was brought before the Inquisition in Rome. There he was forced to renounce the idea that the Earth moved around the Sun. The Church insisted that man was at the center of the universe. He was tried for dissent, forced into silence and sentenced to house arrest for the remainder of his life.

Though he had published his support for the new Copernican system as early as 1610, and Pope Pius V had declared it heresy, Galileo was able to juggle his differences with the clergy for twenty-two more years. But in 1632 he published his *Dialogue Concerning the Two World Systems* in which one character maintained that the heavens revolve around man, and the other proposed that we are moving around the Sun. Identifying with the first, the Pope felt Galileo had mocked him, and his standoff with the Church escalated into a major confrontation.

After entering his birth data into my computer, I checked instantly to see what he was integrating when his relationship with the clergy collapsed. I gasped as it came up on the screen — his Progressing Moon entered Scorpio that year.

Almost four centuries after the fact, the sky speaks in yet another way. Dealing with power at that time was part of his own process. Without justifying the Church or blaming Galileo for his suppression, there it is. Scorpio is a compression chamber, the chits were being called in and the loans had come due. Though history was perhaps not working from the assumption of taking personal responsibility for our lives in those days, the tracks of our development remain.

Ironically, both Galileo and the Church were right. The Earth does move around the Sun, but now we discover a process that puts humankind at the center all over again. We are each the hub of a holographed sky that guides our unfoldment as Beings. By opposing astrology now, the Church rejects even the poetic justice that would have come down on their side this time.

As Christianity prepares to enter its third millennium, however, Pope John Paul II made repentance of past errors a priority for Catholics, and in 1992 the Church acknowledged Galileo's suffering and that "errors were made." Science and religion have abandoned their disagreement over the shape of our star system, but because of their mutual struggle for understanding, we are a privileged generation. We will know the solar system as both science and religion. Astrology transforms the sky into an experience of spiritual evolution, and unites what we know of both worlds.

Every time I see a panel of journalists discussing current events and history, I want to see a timekeeper there. We have no context at all for the changes we are living through. To astrologers this is like pretending not to know the Sun is at the center of the solar system. We already know what brings on periods of change. We know what the characteristics of history are. We know that nations and people are conditioned by the solar system, and to understand ourselves and our world now, we need to understand time.

RE-TRACKING

One soon begins to realize there are other aspects to this cycle. For one thing, it repeats.

If you are over twenty-eight, you have been once around the track, and the Progressing Moon has begun re-tracing its path.

Though the ongoing clock in the sky and the other progressing planets are always adding new influences, from here on you are treading where you have been before. In a lifetime we have two, sometimes three, experiences of each concept. We saw examples of that when we looked at the nodal axis.

Another way to see what this looks like is to study a country, which of course has a longer history than a person. Astrologers have found that a nation's pattern is set when it declares itself, and since declaring our independence on the Fourth of July in 1776, the United States has integrated its pattern eight times.

The Moon was in Aquarius that day, so we perceive ourselves in an Aquarian, Eleventh House way. That quality jolts, it breaks things loose, it individuates and promotes autonomy, and Americans see themselves as a free and independent people.

Aquarius tunes to real time, the planetary dance, which has a centerpoint, and we ascribe centerpoints to the entire population. We interpret that as equality.

Because the United States' Progressing Moon started out from Aquarius, every time we come back around to it we have another look at who we think we are. At the same time, the Aquarian condition bumps us into synchrony with real time.

That usually feels like sudden change. Since we do not quite live in real time yet, during these periods we make corrections and re-set our course, and Aquarius is associated with reforms. Take a very general look at the most recent two-and-a-half-year periods during which we have processed this frequency as a country.

When we entered Aquarius at the end of 1938, we were in the midst of the biggest social reform in our nation's history. Franklin Roosevelt's New Deal attempted to cope with the Great Depression by putting government to the service of the people.

That Aquarian period lasted through 1940 and probably contributed to our remaining neutral at the beginning of World War II. We did not get involved in the war until after we had completed our national experience of autonomy.

We processed Aquarius again between 1966 and 1968, when social reformer Lyndon Johnson was in the White House. Within his vision for The Great Society, we passed consumer and early environmental protection legislation. During this Aquarian period government again turned to social programs considered beneficial to the general population.

Yet when there is a big difference of opinion between a President and the people, an Aquarian climate supports the people. There was widespread opposition to the war in Vietnam in those years. Though Johnson was a social activist, the war split him from the electorate, and in 1968 he declined to run for a second term.

America was next in Aquarius between 1993 and 1995 when we elected another President identified with reform in Bill Clinton. Again we were concerned with change, this time discussing the size of government and whether it was more responsive to lobbyists than to the people.

During that period, we turned out legislators in mid-term elections we thought were too slow to make changes. Republicans won a majority in both houses of Congress for the first time in forty years. While some called this an earthquake in American politics, it was also our periodic Aquarian revolution.

Because an Aquarian climate operates in real time, in an attempt to get current, reform shows up with it. In the former Soviet Union, Nikita Khrushchev attempted reforms while the Soviets were processing this energy in 1957 and 1958. And during their next Aquarian period between 1984 and 1986, Mikhail Gorbachev initiated the revolutionary ideas of glastnost and perestroika and opened the floodgates for the Soviet Union's imminent transformation.

We are all tracking at roughly the same rate, so at any time we are all generally where we were some twenty-seven-plus years ago. Whatever we were processing when President Kennedy was shot, we all took another pass on it in 1991. About that time the Kennedy family walked through another crisis during the William Kennedy Smith rape trial; Oliver Stone's movie *JFK* came out; and several television dramas revisited the assassination. Events are forever associated for all of us with some part of our own process.

Of course individuals experience re-tracing their patterns, too. After being sent to prison in South Africa, Nelson Mandella was freed exactly one cycle later while processing that part of his birthprint again, precisely twenty-seven years later.

Re-tracking often brings up issues that remain unresolved from the last go-round, so if the first Eighth House experience included some sort of trauma at age five, for instance, we would probably address that idea again while integrating the Eighth House condition at thirty-two.

I know of one person who tried to commit suicide every time she moved through or across from that part of her birthprint.

Integrating the Eighth House idea of *power* brought up rumblings that something disturbing had happened to her when she was very young, which coincided with her first trip through the Eighth House as a child. Now progressing opposite that early experience, this woman is resolving issues of feeling powerless in a group for survivors of incest. In retrospect, she has been coming to terms with power from a very early age.

Sometimes old lovers reappear during second passes through the energy of previous romantic times. If you are re-tracing where you were when you met, he is, too. No wonder couples sometimes re-connect.

At forty-nine, Isabel had been thinking about her boyfriend from the sixties, and after years without contact, he called her as they both re-experienced the conditions that originally brought them together.

At the end of his life, Franklin Roosevelt re-united with Lucy Mercer as each of them re-traced the qualities that generated their affair twenty-seven years before.

Edna married each time she integrated her Fourth House. The sense of self developed there is an experience of home, and physically establishing one became important to her at these times. She interpreted them both as time to get married, and the conditions that encouraged her to marry the first time were there once more when she moved through this part of her birthprint again.

Though the cultural climate will have changed, public figures and entertainers are also likely to re-appear twenty-seven years after entering the public eye. The personal conditions that originally brought them into the limelight come around again, and we who liked them the last time are in similar attitudes once more.

After her live concert in June of 1967, Barbra Streisand waited a full twenty-seven years for the same condition to appear again before giving her next live performance in 1994.

Several runs through your pattern will give you more than one reference for the conditioning you carry, and that helps to clarify the issues that come up. Connecting time with the events it generates establishes a platform from which to develop stewardship over life, no matter what the circumstances are.

Is Astrology Science?

I like to wonder about the natural world, and every once in a while someone will remark to me that I should have studied science. Each time I have heard the same phrase in my head, "I did."

The last time this happened was after a conversation in a delicatessen on Christmas Day. A Jewish friend had invited a Muslim friend of ours and me to attend a Christian church with her. The three of us were having our usual eclectic conversation at lunch afterwards when a man at the next table leaned over to make a comment. It turns out he had worked in the space program on the Mercury project, and I was happy to meet someone with this background. I listened intently while he talked about some of his experiences.

After about twenty minutes he asked me what my interests were. I hesitate to mention to any scientist that I study astrology, but he was a stranger I would never meet again, so I did. He was very gracious, and he asked me if I thought astrology was a science. I asked him to define what he meant by 'science,' and as he was reeling off the necessary parameters, the answer popped into my mind.

The difference between science and astrology is that astrologers study conditions that are not repeatable. While science relies on repeating results to verify them, no such thing exists in time. We cannot repeat an experience to see if the same thing happens twice.

So although astrology feels like science, it is different, perhaps more. These two disciplines live in separate paradigms. Science is how we have come to understand the physical world in the paradigm now passing away. The Piscean Age has *deep understanding* as a basic trait, and we have pursued that not only through The Church, but through research. We developed the scientific method as we began to complete this condition during the last quarter of its 2,000 years.

But astrology is about the experience of real time. Though individual cycles in the solar clock recur, the total mix of planetary conditions never does. Astrologers discover correspondences in lots of ways, but not through repeatability. Our realizations have come from watching a condition play out in continually different combinations.

We have found that 'going-around' contains a generic set of characteristics. We find that each planet consistently delivers these characteristics in one particular manner. Astrologers who study history, for instance, find that generations respond to the motions of Pluto. Art historians would find that trends in art are reflected by Neptune.

When two planets come together, we find their qualities married in our experience. And people who study the stock market find that time influences the flow of money.

Astrologers know that people born at the same time of day have similar ways of actualizing themselves. We find the orientation of a planet in a birth pattern relates to certain traits. And in the research I do, I find that personal growth is in step with the Progressing Moon.

While all of these cycles are consistent by themselves, none of them is separate from the whole, which is always changing. So, no repeatability.

In the next paradigm, whatever we have already learned through science will be re-stated in terms of time. The old information will not necessarily be replaced — it does not just go away. It is transformed when placed within the flow of changing conditions.

Astrology relates everything to these conditions, and I don't concern myself any more with whether or not it is a science.

It is what it is.

TIME AND CREATIVITY

When I stopped working a nine-to-five job, I turned back into a nice person. Wrong work is stressful, and after leaving my job I thought about why it felt so good.

I no longer have to do something I am not interested in — yet, even so, I could do that job without being miserable.

I do not have to be with people who complain — yet I could turn the conversation to other things.

I do not have to go back and forth to the office — still, I enjoyed reading on the bus.

What makes the difference, what really makes doing my own work so satisfying, aside from the work itself, is *being in control of my own time.*

When I realized that, it seemed obvious. Writing and the sessions I do to connect people with this cycle are a creative process, and time and creativity are a polar pair. They require each other. I forgot.

An awareness of time is characteristic of the exciting Aquarian period ahead of us. How very appropriate that controlling one's own time is part of the reformation occurring within the whole labor force as we enter this space. Even if we have not found our

171

right work, flexible work schedules are attempts to gain control of time. More companies are giving their employees options to choose the hours they will be in the office. Some offer opportunities to telecommute. And occasionally two people share a job, the hours to be worked out between them.

But creative work is what we will all be doing eventually, and for this we need to be free. The constraints of 'having a job' are characteristic of the old civilization, while the new one is about 'having time.'

If we can combine these two, we are halfway there, but we have full citizenship in the new paradigm when our time is truly our own.

BEING IN STEP

Though we are often critical of people who change their minds, change is not only appropriate, it is inevitable.

In real time, standing pat is destabilizing, and maintaining a balance now depends on having a handle on the sequence of conditions.

While we may plan to focus on something like achievement or family, we spend most of our lives incorporating other ideas like *will, trust, communication, self perception, creativity* and *choice*. But if you know when these qualities shift, you can pick up on your intuition as it tracks with what comes next.

If you have a partner, it is also wise to know what that person is doing. We are less likely to take our differences personally or to make each other wrong if we know the other person's condition, too.

Travelling position, in fact, is part of what brings people together. Couples are often moving through the same House, or through complementary ones opposite each other in space-time. This is immensely helpful to maintaining harmony. I know one couple travelling in the very same degree, so their lives tend to stay synchronized. When a new condition comes along, they both feel it at pretty much the same time.

But travelling position can also be what pulls people apart, especially if we are unaware of how this works. One partner may want to move or buy a house, while the other may be dealing with a lack of confidence, and both conditions are real. Knowing where in the cycle you are validates each person, and that alone lifts a relationship into a larger context.

There is a real basis for promoting each other's mutual evolution. This is not just a nice philosophy any more. Time offers a way to understand yourself, your partner, and what children are dealing with as they grow up.

The possibilities for a family are electrifying. While one person deals with a difficult aspect, another can learn from the idea being played out there. We can validate someone's experience without making that person wrong. We can encourage each other's growth from a position of objectivity while learning first-hand the qualities of conscious evolution. True self actualization is coming with the Aquarian time.

Time validates friendships, too. As I became more interested in making this research public, a good friend of mine was entering a period of intense retreat. We had to make room for this pull in different directions, but knowing why we were not in quite the same space any more helped. We did not have to make a big issue of it.

Needing to change has very little to do with our circumstances, and everything to do with the cycle already built into our lives. If we can understand we are not only different in *what* interests us, but in *when* we are interested, we can stop judging each other for being so unique.

Yet in the end, no matter how different we are, we are all processing the same cycle here, and we are together as travelers in time.

ARE SPIRITUAL TEACHERS DIFFERENT?

Occasionally someone wants to know whether the patterns of our spiritual teachers are somehow different from ours. I asked this question myself. Is there perhaps something about them by which they transcend their birthprints altogether and are beyond the process the rest of us undergo? The answer is no.

Some time ago I came across research done on this subject, and I regret I do not remember who conducted it. It concluded that whereas we might expect there to be some hidden ingredient, some special circumstance ascribed to people like this that would exempt them from expressing the mundane life most of us experience, in fact almost the opposite is true. The researcher felt such teachers were in fact more like their patterns than most of us.

If what we experience by our resonance with time is meaning, the quality we associate with soul and spiritual attunement, these findings make perfect sense. Blending our will with Being increases our attunement with our spiritual process. By aligning with our intuition, we gain the advantage of the wisdom from whence it comes — and intuition is in touch with time.

Jeddu Krishnamurti is perhaps one of these people. His life was quite a dramatic story. Here is a man who was groomed from the age of twelve, selected in 1907 by members of the Theosophical Society to become the new messiah.

He took his first initiation into this group when he was passing over Jupiter. We relate to this piece of spacetime as if it were already organized into a body of information, and it was then he was absorbed into the Theosophical teachings. Eventually brought from India to California to further prepare for this role, he was accompanied by his brother who was thought to play an essential supporting part.

Yet when Mr. Krishnamurti entered his Twelfth House, where we undergo a re-evaluation, his brother died and his entire philosophy and faith in this mission were badly shaken.

Perhaps the defining moment in his development was his subsequent break from the Theosophists. It came as he entered the First House — during which time all of us begin anew.

Mr. Krishnamurti has his North Node there, which puts a special emphasis on developing the idea of separation and the use of personal *will*. Eight days before crossing that Node, he renounced the role of messiah and issued his manifesto, *Truth is a Pathless Path*. Referring to his position as head of a sub-group called the Order of the Star, he said, "...I have decided, as I happen to be the head of the Order, to dissolve it." Combining the Pisces energy of dissolution which also imprinted in his First House, here is his expression of re-placing the *will* and beginning again, as we all do in this part of the pattern.

Mr. Krishnamurti's continuing message was that each one of us must find Truth for ourselves, and that no organization could provide it for us. To become more of who we already are by following our *individual* way is a deepening of the spiritual process for all of us, and he was not exempt.

When a new frequency approaches, we usually feel it coming, and often a restlessness appears as the new idea comes in. At the same time, the past seems to become more visible as we move beyond its quality, which might feel like being done with something, or bored with it.

Culturally we are done with *sameness*. Sameness is a quality of the Piscean civilization, manifesting, for instance, the politics of organized religion, empire and confederation. There is no perspective to be gained, nor any longer view to be taken, until an idea is done with us.

And now that one is.

Wholeness

One night I tuned into a television program called *Earth From Space*. It showed footage taken by astronauts from so high up the Earth was round, and with the very first image of the whole planet I started to cry. Some astronauts say they have had the same experience.

What is that? Maps don't do that, and looking down from an airplane doesn't do that either. But seeing Earth does something instantly, and when I followed that feeling down into myself I found it rooted in wholeness. Earth is one whole thing and it rings *Being* — like a gong — as no amount of reading about oneness or God or religion does.

Toward the end of the program one astronaut talked about that experience. "You know, when you look at Earth it looks happy. It just looks happy," he said.

And he is right, it does. Maps don't look happy, and down inside this planet we are not happy, either. But Earth contains both north-and-south, day-and-night and male-and-female, and wholeness lives at the planetary level.

In all of history, we are alive to see our planet for the very first time. Planetary consciousness is for us, and it is a happy place.

Whatever circles
Belongs to the center.

— Rumi

APPENDICES

Terms associated with

APPENDIX 1

Terms associated with the FIRST HOUSE: *will*

Focus, separate, initiate, launch, project, hurtle, aim, catapult, bolt, charge, dash, dart, enter, begin, start, commence, verbalize, impel, move, drive, propel, assert, inaugurate, introduce, go out, go forth, exit, eject, depart, do, act, affirm, attest, activate, instigate, insert, interject, excite, march, advance, mobilize, proceed, pursue, chase, propose, declare, avow, compete, declaim, attack, divide, trigger, relocate, race, run, express, present, first, assertive, projective, active, competitive, combative, aggressive, outspoken, positive, forward, ahead, toward, the attention, identity, personal presentation, expression, grimace, look, facade, front, personality, physical body, physique, face, mask, vision, proponent, car, vehicle, bird, machinery, missile, bullet, fire, warrior, advocate, champion, athlete, competitor, competition, contest, military, army, red, iron, body, head, hat, the eyes.

APPENDIX 2

Terms associated with the SECOND HOUSE: *trust*

Have, own, establish, value, appreciate, stability, confidence, self esteem, assurance, poise, commitment, self sufficiency, self worth, reliance, assurance, security, collateral, deposit, certainty, surety, guarantee, promise, benefit, resource, talent, aptitude, assets, belongings, economics, money, currency, endowment, bank, depository, treasury, finance, gourmet, gourmand, farmer, banker, financier, farm, garden, possessions, food, sustenance, provisions, fodder, the senses, sensual, stable, material, substantial, permanent, firm, steadfast, trustworthy, dependable, solid, steady, constant, fixed, secure, sturdy, committed, reliable, throat, the voice.

APPENDIX 3

Terms associated with the THIRD HOUSE: *communication*

Connect, link, bridge, span, associate, communicate, converse, correspond, exchange, barter, trade, write, transcribe, scribble, talk, discuss, visit, chatter, gossip, utter, read, environment, neighborhood, siblings, neighbors, surroundings, vicinity, community, city, metropolis, association, atmosphere, circumstances, commerce, information, libraries, news, newspaper, mail, tidings, dispatch, report, data, conversation, discussion, oration, rumor, jargon, correspondence, telephone, telegraph, messenger, courier, reporter, emissary, periodical, newspaper, letter, short trips, tour, junket, shuttle, early education, diversity, assortment, multiplicity, variety, metropolitan, dilettante, mercurial, various, diverse, versatile, variable, changeable, eclectic, multifaceted, adaptable, compliant, flexible, facile, glib, debonair, sophisticated, urbane, civic, civil, nervous system, dendrites, the hands.

APPENDIX 4

Terms associated with the FOURTH HOUSE: *Self perception*

Perceive, include, integrate, enclose, contain, comprise, envelop, encompass, incorporate, retain, inhabit, comprehend, hold, nurture, nourish, tend, nurse, sustain, wisdom, perception, integrity, Self, whole, foundation, support, base, enclosure, spread, place, capacity, personal space, abode, domicile, dwelling, residence, lodging, habitat, household, memory, recall, roots, genealogy, habits, feelings, mother, home, family, clan, homeland, room, chamber, land, heritage, lineage, ancestry, inclusive, authentic, genuine, integrative, domestic, indigenous, inherent, stomach, uterus, the breasts, silver.

APPENDIX 5

Terms associated with the FIFTH HOUSE: *creativity*

Create, originate, formulate, produce, behave, be, play, frolic, romp, perform, entertain, dramatize, preen, behavior, conduct, self expression, nobility, purpose, courage, dignity, heartspace, self actualization, strength, valor, children, lover, drama, show, skit, amusement, centerpoint, hub, nucleus, royalty, king, monarch, sovereign, vitality, vigor, pride, playful, frisky, childlike, expressive, sunny, heart, blood, the back, gold.

APPENDIX 6

Terms associated with the SIXTH HOUSE: *choice*

Process, ground, choose, select, order, analyze, evaluate, assess, perfect, assimilate, adjust, remediate, fix, assemble, discriminate, discern, critique, differentiate, refine, hone, clean, prepare, rehearse, practice, train, decide, prefer, distinguish, cull, pick, arrange, classify, organize, systematize, appraise, measure, polish, digest, ingest, metabolize, calibrate, correct, regulate, tune, alter, modify, accommodate, adapt, rectify, maintain, mend, repair, criticize, improve, launder, assist, precision, mastery, competence, service, technique, procedure, technology, means, mechanism, operation, workings, efficiency, health, diet, skill, craft, apprentice, disciple, details, accuracy, proficiency, capability, expertise, routine, policy, strategy, program, options, flicker, puzzle, computer, monk, virgin, worker, assistant, devotee, immaculate, impeccable, pristine, pure, humble, modest, tidy, neat, orderly, sanitary, spotless, unpolluted, chaste, sterile, personal crisis, right work, the intestines.

APPENDIX 7

Terms associated with the SEVENTH HOUSE: *reflection*

Reflect, respond, receive, reply, return, listen, hear, balance, harmonize, blend, mirror, echo, react, accommodate, equalize, compare, weigh, counterbalance, cooperate, reciprocate, agreement, accord, compatibility, harmony, symmetry, relationship, partner, other, alien, woman, associate, companion, complement, cohort, accomplice, adversary, opponent, diplomacy, protocol, tact, decorum, armistice, truce, peace, deference, the arts, color, fashion, design, grace, ritual, ceremony, the dance, rites, harmonious, receptive, graceful, balanced, beautiful, pretty, charming, aesthetic, acquiescent, agreeable, yielding, deferential, copper, the kidneys, the ears.

APPENDIX 8

Terms Associated with the EIGHTH HOUSE: *power*

Implode, collapse, strip, isolate, concentrate, eliminate, purge, purify, extract, align, merge, fuse, refine, reveal, restructure, redefine, re-identify, polarize, reclaim, redeem, regenerate, transmute, transform, evolve, attract, want, desire, envy, betray, take, consume, confront, control, seduce, manipulate, withhold, force, dominate, coerce, claim, steal, kidnap, violate, rape, lose, destroy, pressure, crucible, magnetism, black hole, survival, motivation, essence, seed, encapsulation, union, alchemy, metamorphosis, perestroika, rejuvenation, psychology, radiation, nuclear energy, laser, investment, business, wealth, politics, taxes, interest, debt, immigrants, volcano, passion, jealousy, scandal, treason, obsession, compulsion, sex, risk, danger, emergency, crisis, fear, defense, venom, security, waste, shit, resentment, hostage, violence, the underworld, crime, the edge, life and death, deep, dark, hidden, secret, sultry, intimate, urgent, intense, determined, defiant, tenacious, catastrophic, motivated, toxic, corrupt, stinging, painful, snake, scorpion, colon, reproductive organs, the genitals.

APPENDIX 9

Terms associated with the NINTH HOUSE: *expansion*

Give, inform, permeate, pervade, increase, teach, learn, expand, explore, travel, discover, disseminate, paradigm, system, discovery, philosophy, metaphysics, higher education, organized religion, social system, the far horizons, migration, the outdoors, frontier, wilderness, adventure, games, sports, parks, publishing, broadcasting, networking, storytelling, advertising, sales, public relations, law, the legal system, music, overestimation, more, overextension, inflation, dissipation, ministers, rabbis, explorers, lawyers, professionals, benevolent, gregarious, generous, bountiful, ample, plentiful, expansive, easy, obese, showy, distended, pious, sciatic nerve, the legs.

APPENDIX 10

Terms associated with the TENTH HOUSE: *acknowledgement*

Observe, recognize, confirm, validate, acknowledge, witness, oversee, administrate, govern, direct, manage, judge, save, conserve, reserve, care for, define, precipitate, manifest, crystalize, structure, responsibility, definition, knowledge, authority, hierarchy, discipline, career, achievement, stewardship, form, architecture, government, safety, house, boundary, wall, rules, reality, duty, history, time, hyperspace, the past, the establishment, quality, the father, grandfather, reputation, renown, stone, crystal, condensation, karma, weight, wool, silk, sculpture, arthritis, public, formal, traditional, orthodox, standard, correct, best, classical, excellent, authoritarian, judgmental, superior, arrogant, righteous, serious, grave, rock, lead, teeth, bones, skeleton, hair, protein, the knees.

APPENDIX 11

Terms associated with the ELEVENTH HOUSE: *truth*

___

Liberate, free, awaken, intuit, individuate, innovate, invent, rebel, revolt, change, break away, autonomy, sovereignty, independence, individuality, originality, uniqueness, peer, friend, club, democracy, humanity, human, rights, civil rights, liberty, freedom, entrepreneur, ingenuity, genius, creative mind, laughter, science, invention, renegade, outlaw, vigilante, anarchy, cartoon, mutiny, riot, bomb, revolution, earthquake, shock, lightning, chi, electricity, electronics, radio, flash, spark, charisma, insight, experience, intuition, timing, pacemaker, astrology, different, unusual, brusque, curt, abrupt, sudden, irregular, rare, odd, novel, remarkable, extraordinary, ingenious, conscious, awake, contrary, dispassionate, detached, liberated, self reliant, free-lance, self contained, altruistic, androgynous, unorthodox, alienated, provocative, the ankles.

APPENDIX 12

Terms associated with the TWELFTH HOUSE: *oneness*

Retreat, dissolve, disperse, disengage, elude, erode, diffuse, vanish, de-focus, release, forgive, re-evaluate, accept, understand, inspire, imagine, theorize, dream, meditate, love, meaning, ethics, morals, mass mind, theory, research, inner space, silence, refuge, communism, immersion, hallucination, delusion, hypnosis, addiction, sleep, trance, deep space, deep water, ocean, flow, possibility, wonder, ecstasy, rapture, hope, faith, forgiveness, surrender, belief, spirit, religion, metaphor, poetry, compassion, romance, fad, glamour, drug, persecution, melancholy, schizophrenia, mental illness, psychiatry, confinement, hospital, asylum, martyr, victim, escape, alcohol, universal, wholeness, unity, sameness, unbounded, global, timeless, ethereal, transcendental, spiritual, transparent, invisible, unreal, enchanted, fantastic, symbolic, elegant, vulnerable, sensitive, impressionable, aura, illusion, photography, image, film, theater, priest, mystic, monk, sanctuary, cathedral, monastery, angel, fairy, large animals, whale, horse, elephant, rain forest, tree, jungle, the feet.

APPENDIX 13

Terms Associated with MARS

Focus, separate, initiate, launch, project, hurtle, aim, catapult, bolt, charge, dash, dart, enter, begin, start, commence, verbalize, impel, move, drive, propel, assert, inaugurate, introduce, go out, go forth, exit, eject, depart, do, act, affirm, attest, activate, instigate, insert, interject, excite, march, advance, mobilize, proceed, pursue, chase, propose, declare, avow, compete, declaim, attack, divide, trigger, relocate, race, run, express, present, first, assertive, projective, active, competitive, combative, aggressive, outspoken, positive, forward, ahead, toward, the attention, identity, personal presentation, expression, grimace, look, facade, front, personality, physical body, physique, face, mask, vision, proponent, car, vehicle, bird, machinery, missile, bullet, fire, warrior, advocate, champion, athlete, competitor, competition, contest, military, army, red, iron, body, head, hat, the eyes.

APPENDIX 14

Terms Associated with VENUS: The Second House Version

Have, own, establish, value, appreciate, stability, confidence, self esteem, assurance, poise, commitment, self sufficiency, self worth, reliance, assurance, security, collateral, deposit, certainty, surety, guarantee, promise, benefit, resource, talent, aptitude, assets, belongings, economics, money, currency, endowment, bank, depository, treasury, finance, gourmet, gourmand, farmer, banker, financier, farm, garden, possessions, food, sustenance, provisions, fodder, the senses, sensual, stable, material, substantial, permanent, firm, steadfast, trustworthy, dependable, solid, steady, constant, fixed, secure, sturdy, committed, reliable, throat, the voice.

APPENDIX 15

Terms Associated with MERCURY

Connect, link, bridge, span, associate, communicate, converse, correspond, exchange, barter, trade, write, transcribe, scribble, talk, discuss, visit, chatter, gossip, utter, read, environment, neighborhood, siblings, neighbors, surroundings, vicinity, community, city, metropolis, association, atmosphere, circumstances, commerce, information, libraries, news, newspaper, mail, tidings, dispatch, report, data, conversation, discussion, oration, rumor, jargon, correspondence, telephone, telegraph, messenger, courier, reporter, emissary, periodical, newspaper, letter, short trips, tour, junket, shuttle, early education, diversity, assortment, multiplicity, variety, metropolitan, dilettante, mercurial, various, diverse, versatile, variable, changeable, eclectic, multifaceted, adaptable, compliant, flexible, facile, glib, debonair, sophisticated, urbane, civic, civil, nervous system, dendrites, the hands.

APPENDIX 16

Terms Associated with THE MOON

Perceive, include, integrate, enclose, contain, comprise, envelop, encompass, incorporate, retain, inhabit, comprehend, hold, nurture, nourish, tend, nurse, sustain, wisdom, perception, integrity, Self, whole, foundation, support, base, enclosure, spread, place, capacity, personal space, abode, domicile, dwelling, residence, lodging, habitat, household, memory, recall, roots, genealogy, habits, feelings, mother, home, family, clan, homeland, room, chamber, land, heritage, lineage, ancestry, inclusive, authentic, genuine, integrative, domestic, indigenous, inherent, stomach, uterus, the breasts, silver.

APPENDIX 17

Terms Associated with THE SUN

Create, originate, formulate, produce, behave, be, play, frolic, romp, perform, entertain, dramatize, preen, behavior, conduct, self expression, nobility, purpose, courage, dignity, heartspace, self actualization, strength, valor, children, lover, drama, show, skit, amusement, centerpoint, hub, nucleus, royalty, king, monarch, sovereign, vitality, vigor, pride, playful, frisky, childlike, expressive, sunny, heart, blood, the back, gold.

APPENDIX 18

Terms Associated with CHIRON

Process, ground, choose, select, order, analyze, evaluate, assess, perfect, assimilate, adjust, remediate, fix, assemble, discriminate, discern, critique, differentiate, refine, hone, clean, prepare, rehearse, practice, train, decide, prefer, distinguish, cull, pick, arrange, classify, organize, systematize, appraise, measure, polish, digest, ingest, metabolize, calibrate, correct, regulate, tune, alter, modify, accommodate, adapt, rectify, maintain, mend, repair, criticize, improve, launder, assist, precision, mastery, competence, service, technique, procedure, technology, means, mechanism, operation, workings, efficiency, health, diet, skill, craft, apprentice, disciple, details, accuracy, proficiency, capability, expertise, routine, policy, strategy, program, options, flicker, puzzle, computer, monk, virgin, worker, assistant, devotee, immaculate, impeccable, pristine, pure, humble, modest, tidy, neat, orderly, sanitary, spotless, unpolluted, chaste, sterile, personal crisis, right work, the intestines.

APPENDIX 19

Terms Associated with VENUS: The Seventh House Version

Reflect, respond, receive, reply, return, listen, hear, balance, harmonize, blend, mirror, echo, react, accommodate, equalize, compare, weigh, counterbalance, cooperate, reciprocate, agreement, accord, compatibility, harmony, symmetry, relationship, partner, other, alien, woman, associate, companion, complement, cohort, accomplice, adversary, opponent, diplomacy, protocol, tact, decorum, armistice, truce, peace, deference, the arts, color, fashion, design, grace, ritual, ceremony, the dance, rites, harmonious, receptive, graceful, balanced, beautiful, pretty, charming, aesthetic, acquiescent, agreeable, yielding, deferential, copper, the kidneys, the ears.

APPENDIX 20

Terms Associated with PLUTO

Implode, collapse, strip, isolate, concentrate, eliminate, purge, purify, extract, align, merge, fuse, refine, reveal, restructure, redefine, re-identify, polarize, reclaim, redeem, regenerate, transmute, transform, evolve, attract, want, desire, envy, betray, take, consume, confront, control, seduce, manipulate, withhold, force, dominate, coerce, claim, steal, kidnap, violate, rape, lose, destroy, pressure, crucible, magnetism, black hole, survival, motivation, essence, seed, encapsulation, union, alchemy, metamorphosis, perestroika, rejuvenation, psychology, radiation, nuclear energy, laser, investment, business, wealth, politics, taxes, interest, debt, immigrants, volcano, passion, jealousy, scandal, treason, obsession, compulsion, sex, risk, danger, emergency, crisis, fear, defense, venom, security, waste, shit, resentment, hostage, violence, the underworld, crime, the edge, life and death, deep, dark, hidden, secret, sultry, intimate, urgent, intense, determined, defiant, tenacious, catastrophic, motivated, toxic, corrupt, stinging, painful, snake, scorpion, colon, reproductive organs, the genitals.

APPENDIX 21

Terms Associated with JUPITER

Give, inform, permeate, pervade, increase, teach, learn, expand, explore, travel, discover, disseminate, paradigm, system, discovery, philosophy, metaphysics, higher education, organized religion, social system, the far horizons, migration, the outdoors, frontier, wilderness, adventure, games, sports, parks, publishing, broadcasting, networking, storytelling, advertising, sales, public relations, law, the legal system, music, overestimation, more, overextension, inflation, dissipation, ministers, rabbis, explorers, lawyers, professionals, benevolent, gregarious, generous, bountiful, ample, plentiful, expansive, easy, obese, showy, distended, pious, sciatic nerve, the legs.

APPENDIX 22

Terms Associated with SATURN

Observe, recognize, confirm, validate, acknowledge, witness, oversee, administrate, govern, direct, manage, judge, save, conserve, reserve, care for, define, precipitate, manifest, crystalize, structure, responsibility, definition, knowledge, authority, hierarchy, discipline, career, achievement, stewardship, form, architecture, government, safety, house, boundary, wall, rules, reality, duty, history, time, hyperspace, the past, the establishment, quality, the father, grandfather, reputation, renown, stone, crystal, condensation, karma, weight, wool, silk, sculpture, arthritis, public, formal, traditional, orthodox, standard, correct, best, classical, excellent, authoritarian, judgmental, superior, arrogant, righteous, serious, grave, rock, lead, teeth, bones, skeleton, hair, protein, the knees.

APPENDIX 23

Terms Associated with URANUS

Liberate, free, awaken, intuit, individuate, innovate, invent, rebel, revolt, change, break away, autonomy, sovereignty, independence, individuality, originality, uniqueness, peer, friend, club, democracy, humanity, human, rights, civil rights, liberty, freedom, entrepreneur, ingenuity, genius, creative mind, laughter, science, invention, renegade, outlaw, vigilante, anarchy, cartoon, mutiny, riot, bomb, revolution, earthquake, shock, lightning, chi, electricity, electronics, radio, flash, spark, charisma, insight, experience, intuition, timing, pacemaker, astrology, different, unusual, brusque, curt, abrupt, sudden, irregular, rare, odd, novel, remarkable, extraordinary, ingenious, conscious, awake, contrary, dispassionate, detached, liberated, self reliant, free-lance, self contained, altruistic, androgynous, unorthodox, alienated, provocative, the ankles.

APPENDIX 24

Terms Associated with NEPTUNE

Retreat, dissolve, disperse, disengage, elude, erode, diffuse, vanish, de-focus, release, forgive, re-evaluate, accept, understand, inspire, imagine, theorize, dream, meditate, love, meaning, ethics, morals, mass mind, theory, research, inner space, silence, refuge, communism, immersion, hallucination, delusion, hypnosis, addiction, sleep, trance, deep space, deep water, ocean, flow, possibility, wonder, ecstasy, rapture, hope, faith, forgiveness, surrender, belief, spirit, religion, metaphor, poetry, compassion, romance, fad, glamour, drug, persecution, melancholy, schizophrenia, mental illness, psychiatry, confinement, hospital, asylum, martyr, victim, escape, alcohol, universal, wholeness, unity, sameness, unbounded, global, timeless, ethereal, transcendental, spiritual, transparent, invisible, unreal, enchanted, fantastic, symbolic, elegant, vulnerable, sensitive, impressionable, aura, illusion, photography, image, film, theater, priest, mystic, monk, sanctuary, cathedral, monastery, angel, fairy, large animals, whale, horse, elephant, rain forest, tree, jungle, the feet.

APPENDIX 25

Terms Associated with ARIES

Focus, separate, initiate, launch, project, hurtle, aim, catapult, bolt, charge, dash, dart, enter, begin, start, commence, verbalize, impel, move, drive, propel, assert, inaugurate, introduce, go out, go forth, exit, eject, depart, do, act, affirm, attest, activate, instigate, insert, interject, excite, march, advance, mobilize, proceed, pursue, chase, propose, declare, avow, compete, declaim, attack, divide, trigger, relocate, race, run, express, present, first, assertive, projective, active, competitive, combative, aggressive, outspoken, positive, forward, ahead, toward, the attention, identity, personal presentation, expression, grimace, look, facade, front, personality, physical body, physique, face, mask, vision, proponent, car, vehicle, bird, machinery, missile, bullet, fire, warrior, advocate, champion, athlete, competitor, competition, contest, military, army, red, iron, body, head, hat, the eyes.

APPENDIX 26

Terms Associated with TAURUS

Have, own, establish, value, appreciate, stability, confidence, self esteem, assurance, poise, commitment, self sufficiency, self worth, reliance, assurance, security, collateral, deposit, certainty, surety, guarantee, promise, benefit, resource, talent, aptitude, assets, belongings, economics, money, currency, endowment, bank, depository, treasury, finance, gourmet, gourmand, farmer, banker, financier, farm, garden, possessions, food, sustenance, provisions, fodder, the senses, sensual, stable, material, substantial, permanent, firm, steadfast, trustworthy, dependable, solid, steady, constant, fixed, secure, sturdy, committed, reliable, throat, the voice.

APPENDIX 27

Terms Associated with GEMINI

Connect, link, bridge, span, associate, communicate, converse, correspond, exchange, barter, trade, write, transcribe, scribble, talk, discuss, visit, chatter, gossip, utter, read, environment, neighborhood, siblings, neighbors, surroundings, vicinity, community, city, metropolis, association, atmosphere, circumstances, commerce, information, libraries, news, newspaper, mail, tidings, dispatch, report, data, conversation, discussion, oration, rumor, jargon, correspondence, telephone, telegraph, messenger, courier, reporter, emissary, periodical, newspaper, letter, short trips, tour, junket, shuttle, early education, diversity, assortment, multiplicity, variety, metropolitan, dilettante, mercurial, various, diverse, versatile, variable, changeable, eclectic, multifaceted, adaptable, compliant, flexible, facile, glib, debonair, sophisticated, urbane, civic, civil, nervous system, dendrites, the hands.

APPENDIX 28

Terms Associated with CANCER

Perceive, include, integrate, enclose, contain, comprise, envelop, encompass, incorporate, retain, inhabit, comprehend, hold, nurture, nourish, tend, nurse, sustain, wisdom, perception, integrity, Self, whole, foundation, support, base, enclosure, spread, place, capacity, personal space, abode, domicile, dwelling, residence, lodging, habitat, household, memory, recall, roots, genealogy, habits, feelings, mother, home, family, clan, homeland, room, chamber, land, heritage, lineage, ancestry, inclusive, authentic, genuine, integrative, domestic, indigenous, inherent, stomach, uterus, the breasts, silver.

APPENDIX 29

Terms Associated with LEO

Create, originate, formulate, produce, behave, be, play, frolic, romp, perform, entertain, dramatize, preen, behavior, conduct, self expression, nobility, purpose, courage, dignity, heartspace, self actualization, strength, valor, children, lover, drama, show, skit, amusement, centerpoint, hub, nucleus, royalty, king, monarch, sovereign, vitality, vigor, pride, playful, frisky, childlike, expressive, sunny, heart, blood, the back, gold.

APPENDIX 30

Terms Associated with VIRGO

Process, ground, choose, select, order, analyze, evaluate, assess, perfect, assimilate, adjust, remediate, fix, assemble, discriminate, discern, critique, differentiate, refine, hone, clean, prepare, rehearse, practice, train, decide, prefer, distinguish, cull, pick, arrange, classify, organize, systematize, appraise, measure, polish, digest, ingest, metabolize, calibrate, correct, regulate, tune, alter, modify, accommodate, adapt, rectify, maintain, mend, repair, criticize, improve, launder, assist, precision, mastery, competence, service, technique, procedure, technology, means, mechanism, operation, workings, efficiency, health, diet, skill, craft, apprentice, disciple, details, accuracy, proficiency, capability, expertise, routine, policy, strategy, program, options, flicker, puzzle, computer, monk, virgin, worker, assistant, devotee, immaculate, impeccable, pristine, pure, humble, modest, tidy, neat, orderly, sanitary, spotless, unpolluted, chaste, sterile, personal crisis, right work, the intestines.

APPENDIX 31

Terms Associated with LIBRA

Reflect, respond, receive, reply, return, listen, hear, balance, harmonize, blend, mirror, echo, react, accommodate, equalize, compare, weigh, counterbalance, cooperate, reciprocate, agreement, accord, compatibility, harmony, symmetry, relationship, partner, other, alien, woman, associate, companion, complement, cohort, accomplice, adversary, opponent, diplomacy, protocol, tact, decorum, armistice, truce, peace, deference, the arts, color, fashion, design, grace, ritual, ceremony, the dance, rites, harmonious, receptive, graceful, balanced, beautiful, pretty, charming, aesthetic, acquiescent, agreeable, yielding, deferential, copper, the kidneys, the ears.

APPENDIX 32

Terms Associated with SCORPIO

Implode, collapse, strip, isolate, concentrate, eliminate, purge, purify, extract, align, merge, fuse, refine, reveal, restructure, redefine, re-identify, polarize, reclaim, redeem, regenerate, transmute, transform, evolve, attract, want, desire, envy, betray, take, consume, confront, control, seduce, manipulate, withhold, force, dominate, coerce, claim, steal, kidnap, violate, rape, lose, destroy, pressure, crucible, magnetism, black hole, survival, motivation, essence, seed, encapsulation, union, alchemy, metamorphosis, perestroika, rejuvenation, psychology, radiation, nuclear energy, laser, investment, business, wealth, politics, taxes, interest, debt, immigrants, volcano, passion, jealousy, scandal, treason, obsession, compulsion, sex, risk, danger, emergency, crisis, fear, defense, venom, security, waste, shit, resentment, hostage, violence, the underworld, crime, the edge, life and death, deep, dark, hidden, secret, sultry, intimate, urgent, intense, determined, defiant, tenacious, catastrophic, motivated, toxic, corrupt, stinging, painful, snake, scorpion, colon, reproductive organs, the genitals.

APPENDIX 33

Terms Associated with SAGITTARIUS

Give, inform, permeate, pervade, increase, teach, learn, expand, explore, travel, discover, disseminate, paradigm, system, discovery, philosophy, metaphysics, higher education, organized religion, social system, the far horizons, migration, the outdoors, frontier, wilderness, adventure, games, sports, parks, publishing, broadcasting, networking, storytelling, advertising, sales, public relations, law, the legal system, music, overestimation, more, overextension, inflation, dissipation, ministers, rabbis, explorers, lawyers, professionals, benevolent, gregarious, generous, bountiful, ample, plentiful, expansive, easy, obese, showy, distended, pious, sciatic nerve, the legs.

APPENDIX 34

Terms Associated wit CAPRICORN

Observe, recognize, confirm, validate, acknowledge, witness, oversee, administrate, govern, direct, manage, judge, save, conserve, reserve, care for, define, precipitate, manifest, crystalize, structure, responsibility, definition, knowledge, authority, hierarchy, discipline, career, achievement, stewardship, form, architecture, government, safety, house, boundary, wall, rules, reality, duty, history, time, hyperspace, the past, the establishment, quality, the father, grandfather, reputation, renown, stone, crystal, condensation, karma, weight, wool, silk, sculpture, arthritis, public, formal, traditional, orthodox, standard, correct, best, classical, excellent, authoritarian, judgmental, superior, arrogant, righteous, serious, grave, rock, lead, teeth, bones, skeleton, hair, protein, the knees.

APPENDIX 35

Terms Associated with AQUARIUS

Liberate, free, awaken, intuit, individuate, innovate, invent, rebel, revolt, change, break away, autonomy, sovereignty, independence, individuality, originality, uniqueness, peer, friend, club, democracy, humanity, human, rights, civil rights, liberty, freedom, entrepreneur, ingenuity, genius, creative mind, laughter, science, invention, renegade, outlaw, vigilante, anarchy, cartoon, mutiny, riot, bomb, revolution, earthquake, shock, lightning, chi, electricity, electronics, radio, flash, spark, charisma, insight, experience, intuition, timing, pacemaker, astrology, different, unusual, brusque, curt, abrupt, sudden, irregular, rare, odd, novel, remarkable, extraordinary, ingenious, conscious, awake, contrary, dispassionate, detached, liberated, self reliant, free-lance, self contained, altruistic, androgynous, unorthodox, alienated, provocative, the ankles.

APPENDIX 36

Terms Associated with PISCES

Retreat, dissolve, disperse, disengage, elude, erode, diffuse, vanish, de-focus, release, forgive, re-evaluate, accept, understand, inspire, imagine, theorize, dream, meditate, love, meaning, ethics, morals, mass mind, theory, research, inner space, silence, refuge, communism, immersion, hallucination, delusion, hypnosis, addiction, sleep, trance, deep space, deep water, ocean, flow, possibility, wonder, ecstasy, rapture, hope, faith, forgiveness, surrender, belief, spirit, religion, metaphor, poetry, compassion, romance, fad, glamour, drug, persecution, melancholy, schizophrenia, mental illness, psychiatry, confinement, hospital, asylum, martyr, victim, escape, alcohol, universal, wholeness, unity, sameness, unbounded, global, timeless, ethereal, transcendental, spiritual, transparent, invisible, unreal, enchanted, fantastic, symbolic, elegant, vulnerable, sensitive, impressionable, aura, illusion, photography, image, film, theater, priest, mystic, monk, sanctuary, cathedral, monastery, angel, fairy, large animals, whale, horse, elephant, rain forest, tree, jungle, the feet.

ACKNOWLEDGEMENTS

Thank you to all the people who have shared their lives with me through *Locating Yourself In Time*. What I have learned from you all has allowed me to understand this process.

Thank you to Victoria Neal for her comments, and to Laurel Airica for her poetic and professional counsel.

ABOUT THE AUTHOR

Marianna Porter has been studying the characteristics of time since 1980. She has written a series of articles and is currently studying the generations of the Twentieth Century.

She lives in Los Angeles at 118°20 west and 34°03 north and teaches through her practice *Locating Yourself In Time*.

HOW TO REACH THE AUTHOR

If you have your birth time and place, we can calculate just when you process each House and fix a date to the integration of every planet. To connect yourself with this cycle, contact the author at Clary Press to arrange a session.

Or to simply learn more about a session, request information about *Locating Yourself in Time.*

Clary Press
P.O. Box 480702
Building B
Los Angeles, CA 90048-9302

SEND OUT ANOTHER COPY.

Please send a copy of this book to the person below. I enclose a check for $19.95 ($17.95 + $2 s/h) made out to Clary Press.

Your copy is on its way.

Send *The Earth Game* to:

Name _____

Address _____

City _____

State _____ ZIP _____

Mail your check to:

Clary Press
P.O. Box 480702
Building B
Los Angeles, CA 90048-9302